The Complete Book of

wok

Cooking

The Complete Book of

wok

Cooking

APPLE

Contents

Recipe list

Rice and noodles

Desserts

Sauces and condiments

Introduction

The beauty of stir-fried food is not just that the dishes are quick to prepare and an extremely energy-efficient way to cook. Nor is it that the most tantalizing aromas are released when the ingredients mingle and sizzle during cooking, although this is quite wonderful. This method beats all others simply because it seals in the flavors and nutrients of the foods and preserves their original color and textures, making meals tasty, satisfying and healthy.

Stir-frying is the most popular way to cook food in Asia. The technique originated from China and over the centuries it was adopted throughout Asian kitchens. Vietnamese cuisine, for example, is a fusion of the best culinary elements of China's traditions with its use of chopsticks and woks, stir-fried dishes and plethora of noodles. Today, stir-frying has well and truly conquered the world, used frequently by Western chefs and home cooks alike.

With only four of the most ancient and rudimentary implements—cleaver, board, wok and spatula—plus a source of intense heat, stir-fries are easy to prepare. The success in cooking depends on having all the ingredients ready before cooking starts. The ingredients should be cut into pieces of about the same size, and the meat and poultry cut across the grain (partially frozen meat is easier to slice) to ensure they don't become tough during cooking. The food is then cooked in a wok or frying pan with very little oil over a high heat, constantly turning the ingredients.

The wok provides many other easy and effective ways to prepare foods. With a wok you can also steam, boil, braise and deep-fry. In this book we provide a number of recipes that use the wok in these versatile fashions. For example, desserts couldn't be simpler than using a wok with a bamboo steamer, and there is very little that needs cleaning up afterwards. So be adventurous with your wok and you'll find the rewards are more than the tasty food you prepare.

Recipes for stir-fries can often be adapted to suit whatever the refrigerator yields, a bonus when time and budget are short. A simple family meal can be created by making up two or three dishes using meat or seafood and vegetables. You can contrast the dishes by making one mild and one more highly seasoned. Steamed white rice usually accompanies stir-fried dishes, but you may choose to add interest to the rice by stirring in cooked green peas, baby shrimp (prawns) and chopped scallions (spring onions). You can also use noodles instead of rice, whatever you prefer.

When eating stir-fries, serve with Chinese-style tableware—bowls and chopsticks—as these add to the relaxed ambience this style of cooking affords. Tea is one of the best drinks to accompany stir-fries—try the lighter green teas, and plain or scented teas with jasmine blossoms are refreshing—as they cleanse the palate to enable you to enjoy the characteristics of each dish.

As a method of cooking it's obvious that stir-frying has several advantages: the ingredients can be prepared in advance to make cooking time no more than a few minutes, the dishes are economical to make, and the quick cooking ensures minimum loss of nutrients. Since stir-fried dishes cook quickly, they should be cooked just before serving so they are fresh and piping hot.

Enjoy!

Equipment

The wok

The wok is synonymous with stir-fries. The word wok simply means "cooking vessel" in Cantonese—an indication of how versatile and, indeed, indispensable this piece of equipment is for Asian cooks. Its shape, which has remained unchanged for centuries, was originally dictated by the Chinese stove. The stove had an opening in the top into which the round-bottomed wok securely fit.

A wok is a wonderful and practical addition to the contemporary kitchen. The shape accommodates small or large quantities of ingredients and allows control over how they are cooked. The large cooking surface evenly and efficiently conducts and holds heat, making a wok especially well suited for stir-frying. There are few ingredients that cannot be cooked in a wok, whether a recipe is Asian or Western in style.

Of the many woks available, all are basically bowl shaped with gently sloping sides. Some have looped handles on opposite sides; others have a long wooden handle on one side. Woks were traditionally made from cast iron and therefore were quite heavy. They are now available in many different materials and finishes. Carbon or rolled steel is one of the best materials. Nonstick woks are easy to clean but may not promote browning of foods as thoroughly as those made of rolled or carbon steel. Other options include stainless steel woks and electric woks, which may not reach temperatures as high as those of cast iron or carbon steel. Round-bottomed woks work best on gas stoves. A stand may be necessary to provide stability; the best choice is a stand with large perforations that promote good heat circulation. Flat-bottomed woks are suited for electric stove tops because they sit directly and securely on the heating element.

Woks are available in a range of sizes. A wok with a diameter of 14 inches (35 cm) is a versatile size appropriate for the recipes in this book and for other dishes that yield four to six servings. If you don't have a wok, use a large frying pan, a cast-iron skillet, or a russe.

Left: Carbon steel wok

Pictured opposite
Clockwise from top left: electric wok, stainless steel wok, cast iron wok, frying pan, nonstick woks

Preparing a new wok

Woks of carbon steel or rolled steel, the popular inexpensive vessels sold in Asian stores, are coated with a thin film of lacquer to prevent rusting. The film needs to be removed before a wok can be used. The best way to do this is to place the wok on the stove top, fill with cold water and add 2 tablespoons of baking soda (bicarbonate of soda). Bring to a boil and boil rapidly for 15 minutes. Drain and scrub off the coating with a nylon pad. Repeat the process if any coating remains. Then rinse and dry the wok. It is now ready to be seasoned.

Carbon steel, rolled steel and cast iron woks require seasoning before use, which creates a smooth surface that keeps food from sticking to it and prevents it from discoloring.

1 To season a wok: Wipe the wok lightly with oil and place it over high heat until smoking. Immediately plunge it into hot water, then return to heat to dry. Wipe again with oil and repeat these steps three times. At no time should you use soap.

2 To keep a wok clean: Rinse with hot water immediately after use and scour with a plastic or nonmetallic brush. Never use soap, or you will need to season the wok all over again. Do not wipe dry, but place over a low heat to dry. Wipe lightly with oil and store.

3 To heat a wok: Because of the wok's conical shape, a gas flame is preferable to electric as it disperses the heat upward along the sides of the wok. Gas also allows instant regulation of the heat.

4 To cook with a wok: Always preheat the wok before adding any ingredients, including oil. After adding oil, rotate the wok to spread the oil evenly up the sides, then heat before adding anything else.

Versatile cooking methods with a wok

Deep-frying: The wok is ideal for deep-frying as it uses less oil than a deep fryer and can accommodate ingredients without crowding. Make sure the wok is secure on its stand or heating element before adding the oil. Pour the oil into the wok and heat until it reaches 375°F (190°C) on a deep-frying thermometer or until a cube of bread sizzles and turns golden when dropped into the hot oil.

Steaming: This method cooks foods by moist heat supplied by steadily boiling water. A bamboo steamer set over but not touching simmering water in a wok is ideal for cooking buns, dumplings, fish, vegetables and puddings. Half fill the wok with water (the steamer should not touch the water) and bring to a boil. Arrange the food in the steamer, cover, place the steamer in the wok and steam for the required time, adding more water when necessary.

Boiling: A wok can serve as a saucepan, a frying pan and a stewing pot, suitable for simmering a delicate coconut sauce, boiling vegetables, simmering a soup or reducing a sauce.

Braising: Meat or seafood can be browned to seal in the juices. Once liquid is added, the wok can be covered for slow simmering.

Other useful kitchen equipment

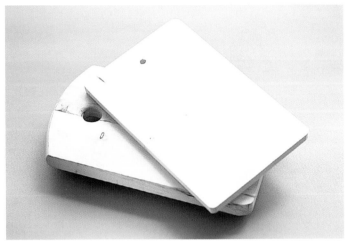

Electric rice cookers are rapidly replacing conventional saucepan cooking. They cook rice perfectly and keep it warm throughout a meal. A saucepan with a tight-fitting lid also produces excellent results.

A good hardwood board is indispensable for proper cutting and other preparations. After use, cutting boards may be scraped clean with the back edge of the cleaver, rinsed with warm water, and hung to dry.

A good cleaver is the most versatile implement in the kitchen. It can cut, chop, slice, shred, mince (grind), pound, peel, scrape, flatten, and otherwise process every type of ingredient. A light cleaver is good for fine cuts such as shredding and mincing (grinding) and a heavy cleaver can be used for chopping through meat with bone. A properly used and cared-for cleaver will last a lifetime. Steel is best for heavy choppers, but iron is infinitely superior for lighter cleavers used in most cutting. Stainless steel cleavers tend to lose their edge quickly.

The two-level bamboo steamer is one of the cheapest and most attractive utensils for steaming. It is available in many sizes from Asian supermarkets and specialty cookware shops. The open-slat base allows steam to circulate easily and efficiently. The lid has an almost perfect design, allowing excess steam to escape through the tightly woven bamboo, with little condensed steam dripping back onto the food.

Wooden and metal wok spatulas or shovels are used for lifting and stirring foods in the wok. They are designed with a rounded end, facilitating scraping along the contours of the wok. If unavailable, use any wooden or metal spatula or pancake turner.

Mortar and pestles are essential for preparing traditional curry pastes. Their weight is ideal for pulverizing fibrous herbs and spices. Substitute with a food processor.

Cooking chopsticks are a jumbo version of the smaller type used for eating. They are long enough to reach into a wok without getting the hands burned or spattered. They are useful for plucking, arranging, stirring, turning, testing, and otherwise manipulating various types of food in the kitchen.

Electric spice grinders can be used in lieu of a mortar and pestle. Some grinders have both dry and wet mix attachments. You can use a coffee grinder (kept only for spices), but they do not have the two settings. For wet spice mixes, you will need to use a spice grinder to first grind dry spices and then a small food processor to finish the spice mix with the fresh or wet ingredients.

Ingredients

Today's cook can make superb use of an extensive array of ingredients. Each culture's culinary style seems to favor specific foods for its recipes. Basil, garlic, and chili are a popular combination for Thai cooking. The Vietnamese love garlic and coriander. The Chinese prefer a subtle blending of sweet and sour, hence the use of lemongrass, ginger, and star anise. The opportunities to create new flavors are endless—there's a whole world of ingredients to explore. Here are some of the ones we use in this book, but don't forget to look at the glossary for more choices.

Bay leaves

Dried leaves from a large, evergreen tree belonging to the laurel family, and native to the Mediterranean region. The leaves impart a lemon-nutmeg flavor. They are used in cooking, but are not edible.

Bean sprouts

These sprouting green mung beans are sold fresh or canned. Fresh sprouts tend to have a crisper texture and a more delicate flavor. Store in the refrigerator for up to 3 days.

Bok choy

Asian variety of cabbage with thick white stalks and mild-flavored dark green leaves. Sizes of bunches vary, from longer than celery stalks to baby bok choy about 6 inches (15 cm) long. Also known as Chinese cabbage. If unavailable, use Chinese broccoli or choy sum.

Cardamom

This member of the ginger family produces pods that contain seeds with a strong lemony flavor. It is available ground but for best flavor, grind your own just before using.

Cilantro (coriander)

These pungent, fragrant leaves from the coriander plant resemble parsley and are also called Chinese parsley and coriander. They have a sharp, tangy, fresh flavor and aroma. The leaves, stems, and roots are all essential seasonings in Asian cooking.

Chili oil

Spicy oil produced by steeping dried red chilies in oil. Use this hot oil only by the drop. Store in refrigerator after opening.

Chilies

Fresh chilies are available in a combination of sizes and are either red or green. The seeds and membranes are the "hot" parts, so if you prefer less heat in your food remove them before chopping or grinding. You could also reduce (or add) the amount of chilies used in a recipe. Chilies are also available dried.

Chili powder

Made from the long Thai chili, chili powder is not as piquant as cayenne pepper, nor is it the equivalent to Mexican chili powder, which is a combination of spices. When unavailable, use red chili flakes ground to a powder in a mortar or a food processor.

Choy sum

Popular and widely available Chinese green with yellow flowers and thin stalks. Every part of this mild-flavored vegetable can be used. Also known as flowering cabbage.

Daikon

This giant white radish, eaten in a variety of forms as an aid to digestion, is enormously popular in Japan and suits stir-fry dishes perfectly.

Galangal

A rhizome with a sharp flavor, sometimes called Thai ginger, it has reddish skin, orange or white flesh and a peppery gingerlike flavor. Fresh galangal should be peeled before use, then sliced or grated. It is also available dried.

Garlic

This edible bulb is indispensable in innumerable dishes. It goes well with meat, especially lamb, and many vegetables. If you find peeling a garlic clove a problem, simply drop them in boiling water for a few seconds, drain and then run cold water over them. You should be able to just slip off the skins afterwards.

Ginger

Thick rootlike rhizome of the ginger plant, a tall flowering tropical plant native to China. It has a sharp pungent flavor. Once the tan skin is peeled from fresh ginger, the ivory to greenish yellow flesh is grated or sliced. Used fresh in sweet and savory cooking and beverages.

Kaffir lime leaves

Fragrant, shiny, dark green leaves from the kaffir lime tree used fresh or dried, whole or shredded, for their enticing citrus flavor.

Leek

This member of the onion family looks like a large scallion (shallot/spring onion). Choose small to medium–size leeks with crisp white bottoms and fresh green tops. Store them unwashed in the refrigerator in the vegetable crisper or a plastic bag.

Lemongrass

Pale stalks of a tropical grass that contribute an intense lemon flavor to Southeast Asian dishes. After the green blades are removed, the stalks are bruised or sliced before use.

Noodles

Sold fresh in Asian markets, noodles, especially the thinner version, are more commonly bought from supermarkets in a dried form in packets. Although interchangeable, dried noodles should be soaked for 10 minutes in cold water, then drained before use. Fresh noodles can be used directly from the package. Noodles are made from bean thread, eggs, wheat, buckwheat or rice. Cellophane noodles (pictured) can be deep-fried for a crisp texture and then added to an already cooked stir-fry.

Saffron threads

If pepper is the king of spices, then saffron is the queen. Saffron threads are the dried stigmas from a variety of crocus flower, each of which produces only three stigmas. Harvesting saffron is labor-intensive, making it the most costly spice in the world. Saffron threads are generally soaked in a warm liquid to release their intense gold-yellow color and pungent, earthy aroma and flavor.

Shallots (French shallots)

Resembling clustered tiny onions, shallots are brown, gold or pink to purple in color. The white parts of scallions (shallots/spring onions) may be substituted.

Shiitake mushrooms

These are available fresh or dried. If dried, they should be soaked before use for 30 minutes in several changes of water. The stems are then removed and discarded.

Soy sauce

Made from fermented soybeans and used to enhance the flavor of many dishes, different soy have different tastes. Chinese soy sauce is saltier and stronger in taste than the Japanese style. Keep refrigerated once opened and use within 12 months.

Star anise

Dark brown, star-shaped spice with a flavor similar to aniseed but with more depth and sweetness. It is the dried fruit from a variety of evergreen magnolia tree. Commonly used in Chinese cooking, star anise also makes an appearance in Indian foods.

Tamarind

Tamarind paste and pulp are very sour. The paste, sold in block form, requires dilution in hot water and straining. More convenient is commercially available tamarind pulp, puree or water, sold in jars. Because there can be a difference in sourness between commercial and homemade puree, the quantities required are variable.

Preparing ingredients

Chopping an onion

1 Halve onion lengthwise through root and stem ends.

2 Peel onion by removing outer layers of skin.

3 Slice through each onion half 3 or 4 times, parallel to cut surface, to within ½ inch (12 mm) of root end.

4 Slice 4 or 5 times through onion, without cutting into root end.

5 Finally, cut through previous cuts.

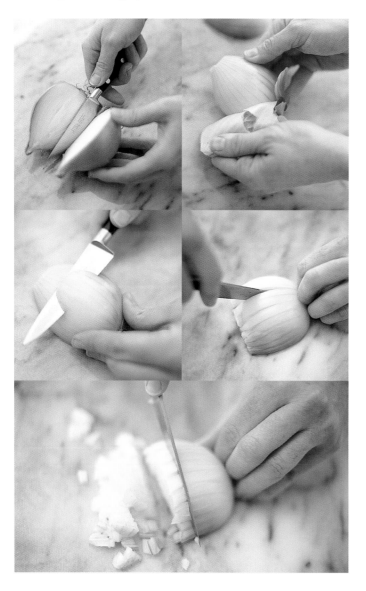

Chopping fresh herbs

Use sharp kitchen shears to snip fresh herbs.

Cutting fine shreds

Paper-thin shreds of herbs are achieved by rolling several leaves together into a tight cylinder, then slicing crosswise. Tender leaves such as basil and mint merely need to be pinched from their stems.

Chili flower

Medium chili

Medium length chilies are ideal for the simplest of chili flowers. Make sure that they are very crisp and fresh, either green or red.

1 Hold the chili flat on a board and use a thin sharp knife to cut lengthwise along the chili from stem to tip. Make about 5 parallel cuts just through the skin to the seeds, but not across them to the other side.

2 Plunge into ice water and the chili "petals" will curl back, while the seed cluster becomes the stamen. If parts of the flower remain closed, prod them gently with the knife and return the flower to the water. These will keep for up to 36 hours if refrigerated in cold water.

Long chili

Long chilies do not blossom as exquisitely as the shorter varieties. To make this garnish, which resembles the beautiful kiriboon flower of Southeast Asia, use a scalpel or preferably a thin V-shaped garnishing knife (available at cookware shops and from some cake-decorating suppliers).

1 Make small V-shaped incisions along the length of the chili, in parallel rows. They should be about ⅛ inch (3 mm) wide and no more than ¼ inch (6 mm) long.

2 Plunge into ice water, as for medium chili, until the incisions curl back like a flower.

Note: For a more spectacular presentation, stick a thin carrot sliver into each of the chiseled holes.

Preparing thick asparagus

If asparagus spears are thick and woody, peeling away tough skin from stalk will result in more tender asparagus after cooking. Using a vegetable peeler or sharp knife, peel away a thin layer of skin beginning at lower part of stem, tapering off progressively as skin becomes more tender toward tip.

Removing corn from a fresh cob

1 Strip corn husks and silk down to stem end of corn.
2 Snap off husks and remove any remaining silk.
3 Grip stem firmly and use a sharp knife to slice away kernels. Slice close to woody cob.

Garnishes

Lemon and lime zest curls

Lemon and lime zest (rind) can be used to garnish and flavor your favorite recipes. Using a citrus zester, firmly scrape the zest from lemons, limes, oranges or grapefruits. If a zester is unavailable, remove zest with a vegetable peeler.

Remove any white pith from zest pieces. Using a very sharp knife, finely slice zest. Place zest in a bowl of ice water. Refrigerate until zest curls, about 15 minutes. (If you are using a zester, it is generally not necessary to place zest in ice water.)

Scallion brushes and curls

1 Using a sharp knife, remove the root section from each scallion (shallot/spring onion). Cut the paler green section into 2-inch (5-cm) sections. Discard the darker green section, or save for another use.
2 To make brushes: Make ¼-inch (6-mm) cuts in each scallion piece, forming a fringe. (Go to step 4.)
3 To make curls: Slice scallion pieces lengthwise into fine strips.
4 Place scallion brushes or strips in a bowl of ice water. Refrigerate until scallions curl, about 15 minutes. Drain and use as garnish.

Toasting seeds, nuts and spices

Because nuts, spices and seeds toast at different times, toast them separately. The general rule is to use your nose: once fragrant, remove from heat immediately. Do not overcook or they may become bitter or acrid.

1 Place nuts, spice or seeds in a dry wok or frying pan over medium heat, and toast, stirring constantly, until lightly golden and fragrant.

2 Alternatively, preheat oven to 400°F (200°C/Gas 6). Spread the nuts, spice or seeds on a rimmed baking pan and toast for 8–12 minutes, shaking the pan once to ensure even browning.

3 If spices need grinding, let cool then grind in a mortar.

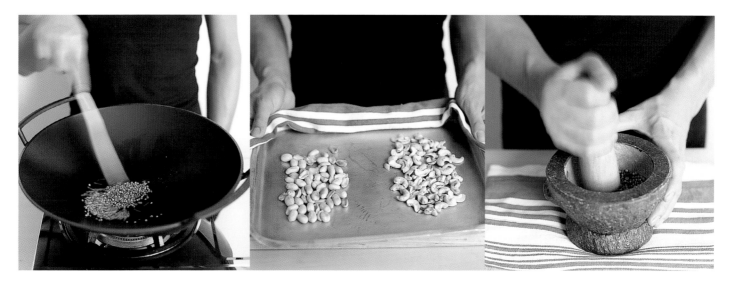

Removing seeds from a tomato

1 Slice tomato in half through stem.
2 Remove seeds, using a teaspoon.

Deseeding a bell pepper (capsicum)

1 If recipe requires a whole bell pepper, slice top off with a sharp knife. If not, cut pepper in half through stem.
2 Using your fingers, remove and discard seeds and white pith from inside bell pepper.

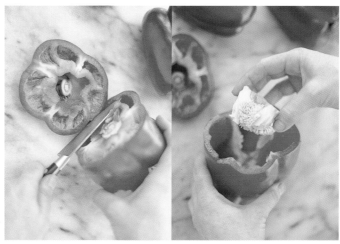

Preparing steamed rice

Though commonly referred to as "steamed rice", standard rice that accompanies most hot and spicy food is actually boiled. When cooked, rice swells to two and half times its volume. Estimate about 1–1½ cups cooked rice per person. If you are using an electric rice cooker follow the manufacturer's directions. If using a saucepan the steps are simple as 1, 2 and 3 below.

1 Rinse rice until the water runs clear, but do not overwork the rice or the grains may break. Drain the rice and put it in a deep, heavy saucepan with a tight-fitting lid.

2 Fill the pan with water to cover the rice by ¾ inch (2 cm). Traditionally, cooks measured by placing their index finger on the rice, adding just enough water to touch their first joint. Do not measure from the pan's bottom, but from the top of the rice. Over high heat, bring the water to a boil and cook until craters form on the rice's surface and the water has disappeared. Immediately cover tightly and reduce heat to a bare simmer. Cook for about 20 minutes, or until tender. Do not lift the lid during the cooking.

3 Use a wooden rice paddle or wooden spoon to fluff the rice up and loosen the grains. If cooking in a nonstick pan, using a bamboo or wooden implement avoids scratching the surface. Serve immediately with your stir-fried dishes.

Cooking noodles

Use the following cooking times as a guide only. Check the noodle package for the manufacturer's recommended cooking times and serving ideas. Always check the noodles during cooking by tasting a strand. Noodles for most dishes should be cooked through. There are basically two ways to cook noodles:

1 Place noodles in a heatproof bowl and cover with boiling water. Soak noodles until soft, then drain. This method is suitable only for fine noodles such as cellophane (bean thread) noodles, rice vermicelli and thin egg noodles.

2 Bring a large saucepan of water to a boil, add noodles and cook until tender, then drain. This method is suitable for all noodles.

Cellophane noodles: These need only be softened in boiling water for 10 minutes; they do not require boiling. Or for a crisp texture, deep-fry them in hot oil until golden and crisp, 1 minute or less.

Egg noodles: If fresh, cook in boiling water for about 3 minutes. If dried, cook in boiling water for about 5 minutes. Some precooked fresh egg noodles need only be soaked in hot water for 8–10 minutes; check package for directions.

Hokkien noodles: Cook in boiling water for 3–4 minutes or stir-fry in hot oil for 3–4 minutes. Some varieties are precooked; check package for directions.

Ramen noodles: Cook in boiling water for about 5 minutes.

Rice stick noodles: Soften dried noodles in hot water for 15 minutes or cook in boiling water for 2–3 minutes. Stir-fry fresh noodles for 2–3 minutes. Some thin rice stick noodles only require soaking in boiling water before adding to soups or stir-fries. Rice vermicelli can be deep-fried to create a crisp "bird's nest" for serving stir-fry dishes.

Soba noodles: If fresh, cook in boiling water for about 1½ minutes. If dried, cook in boiling water for 5–6 minutes.

Somen noodles: Cook in boiling water for about 3 minutes.

Udon noodles: If fresh, cook in boiling water for about 2½ minutes. If dried, cook in boiling water for 10–12 minutes.

Wheat flour noodles: If fresh, cook in boiling water for 3 minutes. If dried, cook in boiling water for 4–5 minutes.

From top: Ramen, somen, udon and soba noodles

appetizers and entrées

Beer-battered prawns with mango salsa

Serves 6–8 as appetizer, 4 as entrée

1 mango, peeled, pitted and chopped

½ cup (2 oz/60 g) chopped scallions
  (shallots/spring onions)

½ small red chili, seeded and chopped

3 tablespoons lime juice

2 teaspoons Asian sesame oil

½ cup (¾ oz/20 g) chopped fresh basil

ground pepper to taste

1½ cups (7½ oz/235 g) all-purpose (plain) flour

1 teaspoon baking powder (bicarbonate of soda)

1 teaspoon salt

½ teaspoon red chili flakes

1 teaspoon brown sugar

1¾ cups (14 fl oz/440 ml) beer

3 cups (24 fl oz/750 ml) vegetable oil for deep-frying

20 jumbo shrimp (king prawns), peeled and
  deveined, tails intact

lime wedges, for serving

To make salsa: In a bowl, combine mango, scallions, chili, lime juice, sesame oil, basil and ground pepper. Mix well and set aside.

Sift flour, baking powder and salt into bowl. Stir in red chili flakes and sugar. Pour in beer and mix with wooden spoon until batter is smooth.

In a wok, heat oil until it reaches 375°F (190°C) on deep-frying thermometer or until a small bread cube dropped in oil sizzles and turns golden. Dip prawns, one at a time, into batter, allow excess to drain off and carefully drop in hot oil. Deep-fry until golden, 30–60 seconds. Using slotted spoon, remove from wok and drain on paper towels. Continue until all prawns are cooked. Serve prawns hot with lime wedges and mango salsa.

Carrot, coconut and ginger soup

Serves 4

1 tablespoon vegetable oil

1 teaspoon Asian sesame oil

1 small red chili, seeded and chopped

4 cloves garlic, crushed

3 teaspoons peeled and grated fresh ginger

2 onions, chopped

2 lb (1 kg) carrots, peeled and sliced

1 teaspoon ground cumin

1 teaspoon ground turmeric

4 cups (32 fl oz/1 L) coconut milk

2 cups (16 fl oz/500 ml) vegetable stock (see page 221)
   or chicken stock (see page 220)

salt and ground pepper to taste

fresh tarragon leaves, for serving

In a wok over a medium heat, warm vegetable and sesame oils. Add chili, garlic and ginger and stir-fry until aromatic, about 1 minute. Add onions, carrots, cumin and turmeric and stir-fry until onions are softened, about 2 minutes.

Pour in coconut milk and stock. Bring to a boil, reduce heat to low and simmer, uncovered, until carrots are tender, 12–15 minutes. Remove from heat.

Working in batches, ladle soup into food processor or blender and process until smooth. Return to wok and heat through for 2 minutes. Taste and season with salt and pepper.

To serve, ladle into individual bowls and garnish with tarragon leaves.

Chicken, spinach and ginger dumplings

Makes 30

1 bunch spinach, stemmed, washed and chopped

8 oz (250 g) ground (minced) chicken

3 scallions (shallots/spring onions), finely chopped

1 teaspoon peeled and grated fresh ginger

2 cloves garlic, crushed

2 teaspoons soy sauce

1 teaspoon Asian sesame oil

½ teaspoon fish sauce

1 small red chili, seeded and finely chopped (optional)

3 teaspoons cornstarch (cornflour)

30 wonton wrappers

¼ cup (2 fl oz/60 ml) rice vinegar

2 tablespoons sugar

2 tablespoons water

1 teaspoon lemon juice

¾ teaspoon fish sauce

1 small red chili, finely chopped (seeds removed
   for milder taste)

Put spinach in a bamboo steamer or steamer basket. Partially fill a wok or pot with water (steamer should not touch water), and bring to a rapid simmer. Put steamer over water, cover, and steam until spinach is soft, 2–3 minutes. Remove from heat and let cool. Squeeze out excess water and chop finely.

In a medium bowl, combine spinach, chicken, scallions, ginger, garlic, soy sauce, sesame oil, fish sauce, chili and cornstarch. Mix well.

Place wonton wrappers on work surface and cover with a damp kitchen towel to prevent them from drying out. Working with 1 wrapper at a time, place 2 teaspoons filling in center and brush edges of wrapper with water. Gather edges together and twist to seal or fold wrapper in half, pressing edges together with fingers to seal. Cover with a damp kitchen towel and set aside. Repeat with remaining wrappers.

Line a large bamboo steamer or steamer basket with parchment (baking) paper. Partially fill a large wok or pot with water (steamer should not touch water) and bring to a rapid simmer. Arrange dumplings in steamer, making sure they do not touch. Place over water, cover, and steam for 10 minutes, adding more simmering water as necessary.

Meanwhile, combine rice vinegar, sugar, water, lemon juice, fish sauce and chili to make dipping sauce. Mix well.

Lift steamer off wok and carefully remove dumplings. Serve warm with dipping sauce.

Chickpea patties

Makes about 30 patties

1½ cups (10 oz/300 g) dried chickpeas
 (garbanzo beans)
4 cups (32 fl oz/1 L) cold water
1 medium yellow (brown) onion, coarsely chopped
2 cloves garlic
6 tablespoons chopped fresh flat-leaf (Italian) parsley
3 tablespoons chopped cilantro (fresh coriander)
pinch ground red chili
1 teaspoon ground coriander
½ teaspoon ground cumin
½ teaspoon baking soda (bicarbonate of soda)
1 teaspoon salt
freshly ground pepper to taste
vegetable oil for deep-frying
tahini sauce (see page 230), for serving

Put chickpeas in a bowl, add water and soak in a cool place for 12–15 hours or overnight.

Drain chickpeas and rinse well. (Do not cook chickpeas as patties would disintegrate when fried).

In a bowl, combine soaked chickpeas with onion, garlic, parsley, cilantro, ground chili, coriander, cumin, baking soda, salt and pepper. Toss ingredients lightly to mix.

In a food processor, process mixture in batches until finely ground. Alternatively, the mixture can be passed through a food grinder twice, using a fine screen.

Place the ground mixture in a bowl and knead well so that it just holds together. Cover and set aside for 30 minutes.

With moistened hands, shape generous tablespoonfuls of mixture into balls, then flatten into thick patties 1½ inches (4 cm) in diameter. Place on a baking sheet and set aside for 15 minutes.

In a wok over medium heat, pour oil to a depth of 1 inch (2.5 cm). When the oil reaches 375°F (190°C) on a deep-frying thermometer, add 6–8 patties at a time and cook, turning once, until deep golden brown, 3–4 minutes. Remove with a slotted spoon and drain on paper towels. Serve hot as an appetizer with tahini sauce.

Tip

Do not use a large onion as this will make the mixture too soft.

Chili-chicken dumplings

Makes 16

8 oz (250 g) ground (minced) chicken

4 scallions (shallots/spring onions), finely chopped

¼ clove garlic, crushed

¼ cup (1½ oz/45 g) roasted peanuts, finely chopped

¼ cup (⅓ oz/10 g) cilantro (fresh coriander) leaves, chopped

1 tablespoon sweet chili sauce

2 teaspoons soy sauce

½ teaspoon fish sauce

16 round wonton or pot sticker (gow gee) wrappers

¼ cup (2 fl oz/60 ml) rice vinegar

¼ cup (2 fl oz/60 ml) fresh lime juice

2 teaspoons fish sauce

1 tablespoon packed palm or brown sugar

1 tablespoon water

1 clove garlic, crushed

1 small fresh red chili, seeded and finely chopped (leave seeds in for more heat)

In a bowl, combine chicken, scallions, garlic, peanuts, cilantro, chili sauce, soy sauce and fish sauce. Place wrappers on a work surface and cover with a damp kitchen towel to prevent them from drying out. Take each wrapper and place in a gow gee press or place 1 wrapper on a work surface. Spoon 2 teaspoons filling in center of wrapper. Brush edges of wrapper with water, and close seal of press, or fold in half, pressing with fingers to seal and make a frilled edge. Cover with a damp kitchen towel and repeat with remaining wrappers and filling.

Place dumplings in a steamer or steamer basket lined with parchment (baking) paper, leaving some space for steam to circulate efficiently. Partially fill a wok or pot with water (steamer or basket should not touch water) and bring to a rapid simmer. Place steamer over boiling water and cover. Steam for 10 minutes.

For chili sauce: In a bowl, combine rice vinegar, lime juice, fish sauce, sugar, water, garlic and chili. Stir constantly until sugar dissolves. Serve dumplings warm with chili sauce.

Cilantro and lime fish cakes

Makes 36 cakes

1 lb (500 g) redfish fillets or skinless, boneless
   white-fleshed fish fillets
1 tablespoon red curry paste (see page 231)
1 tablespoon fish sauce
1 egg, beaten
2 teaspoons brown sugar
1 clove garlic, crushed
4 kaffir lime leaves, finely shredded,
   or 2 teaspoons grated lime zest (rind)
2 tablespoons chopped cilantro (fresh coriander)
2 scallions (shallots/spring onions), finely sliced
½ cup (2½ oz/75 g) finely sliced green beans
3 tablespoons vegetable oil, for frying
12 bamboo skewers
½ cup (4 fl oz/125 ml) light soy sauce, for dipping
lime wedges and extra skewers, for serving

In a food processor, combine fish fillets, curry paste, fish sauce, egg, sugar and garlic. Process until mixture forms a thick paste, about 20 seconds. Transfer to a bowl. Add lime leaves, cilantro, scallions and beans. Using wet hands, mix until well combined. Form mixture into 36 balls. Flatten each to form a patty shape.

In a wok, heat oil over medium heat. Working in batches, fry fish cakes until golden, about 1 minute on each side. Remove fish cakes from pan and drain on paper towels, then place 3 fish cakes on each skewer.

Serve with soy sauce for dipping and fresh lime wedges on skewers for garnish.

Crispy fried wontons with chicken filling

Serves 4

16 oz (500 g) ground (minced) chicken

2 teaspoons peeled and grated fresh ginger

4 scallions (shallots/spring onions), sliced

¼ cup (2 oz/60 g) finely chopped canned
water chestnuts

1 teaspoon Asian sesame oil

2 tablespoons soy sauce

1 tablespoon dry sherry

24 wonton wrappers

vegetable oil, for deep-frying

1 tablespoon light soy sauce

1 teaspoon rice wine

1 teaspoon Asian sesame oil

1 tablespoon finely sliced scallions
(shallots/spring onions)

½ fresh small red chili, seeded and finely
chopped

½ teaspoon chili sauce

In bowl, combine chicken, ginger, scallions, water chestnuts, sesame oil, soy sauce and sherry. Mix well. Place wonton wrappers on work surface and cover with damp kitchen towel to prevent them from drying out. Working with one wrapper at a time, lay it on work surface and place 1 teaspoon filling in middle. Brush edges with water. Gather wonton corners together and twist to seal. Set aside, covered with plastic wrap. Repeat with remaining wonton wrappers.

In a wok or frying pan, heat vegetable oil until it reaches 375°F (190°C) on a deep-frying thermometer or until a small bread cube dropped in oil sizzles and turns golden. Working in batches if necessary, fry filled wontons until golden and crisp, 1–2 minutes. Using slotted spoon, remove from oil and drain on paper towels.

To make dipping sauce: In a bowl, combine soy sauce, rice wine, sesame oil, scallions, chili and chili sauce. Mix well. Pour into serving dish and set aside.

Serve wontons hot with dipping sauce.

Fish balls

Serves 8–10

1½ lb (750 g) white-fleshed fish fillets

6 scallions (shallots/spring onions), chopped

3 tablespoons chopped fresh flat-leaf (Italian) parsley

1 teaspoon chopped fresh dill

1½ cups (3 oz/90 g) soft white bread crumbs,
   or more if needed

1 egg

1 teaspoon salt

freshly ground black pepper

all-purpose (plain) flour for coating

oil, for deep-frying

lemon wedges, for serving

Remove skin and any bones from fillets. Coarsely chop fillets, place in a bowl and stir in scallions, parsley and dill.

Pass the fish mixture through a food grinder using a fine screen, or process to a paste in a food processor in two batches. Return to bowl and add bread crumbs, egg, about 1 teaspoon salt and pepper to taste. Mix to a firm paste, adding more breadcrumbs if needed.

With moistened hands, shape the fish mixture into walnut-sized balls. If time allows, place on a baking sheet and refrigerate until firm, about 30 minutes.

Coat balls with flour. In a heavy wok over medium–high heat, pour oil to a depth of 1½ inches (4 cm). When oil reaches 375°F (190°C) on a deep-frying thermometer or when a small bread cube dropped in oil sizzles and turns golden, add eight balls at a time and cook, turning to brown evenly, for 6–8 minutes. Remove with a slotted spoon and drain on paper towels. Serve hot with lemon wedges.

Fish wraps

Makes 32

1 lb (500 g) firm white-fleshed fish fillets
2 teaspoons peeled and grated fresh ginger
2 tablespoons sweet chili sauce
6 scallions (shallots/spring onions), chopped
1 tablespoon fish sauce
1 egg, beaten
½ cup (1 oz/30 g) fresh white breadcrumbs
2 tablespoons chopped cilantro (fresh coriander)
32 betel leaves
32 toothpicks
½ cup (4 fl oz/125 ml) sweet chili sauce, for dipping

Place fish in a food processor and process until a thick paste is formed, about 30 seconds. Add ginger, chili sauce, scallions, fish sauce, egg, breadcrumbs and cilantro. Process until well combined, about 10 seconds. Using wet hands, divide mixture into 32 portions and shape into balls.

Line a medium-sized bamboo steamer with parchment (baking) paper. Half fill a medium-sized wok with water (steamer should not touch water) and bring water to a boil. Working in batches, arrange fish balls in steamer. Cover, place over boiling water and steam until cooked through, about 15 minutes, adding more water to wok when necessary. Lift steamer from wok and carefully remove fish balls. Wrap each ball in a betel leaf and skewer with a toothpick. Serve warm with chili sauce for dipping.

Tip

Use butter lettuce leaves or basil leaves if betel leaves are unavailable.

Fried chicken wontons

Serves 10–12 as appetizer, 6–8 as entrée

1 tablespoon vegetable oil,
   plus 4 cups (32 fl oz/1 L) oil for deep-frying
1 onion, chopped
1 clove garlic, crushed
8 oz (250 g) ground (minced) chicken
2 tablespoon chunky peanut butter
1 tablespoon sweet chili sauce
1 tablespoon lemon juice
¼ cup (⅓ oz/10 g) chopped cilantro
   (fresh coriander)
48 round wonton wrappers
chili oil, for serving

In a wok over medium–high heat, warm 1 tablespoon vegetable oil. Add onion and garlic and stir-fry until softened, 1–2 minutes. Add chicken and stir-fry until chicken changes color. Remove from heat. Add peanut butter, chili sauce, lemon juice and cilantro. Allow to cool completely.

Place wonton wrappers on work surface and cover with damp kitchen towel to prevent them from drying out. Working with one wrapper at a time, lay it on work surface and place 1 heaped teaspoon chicken filling in middle. Brush edges with water. Place another wonton wrapper on top and firmly press edges together. Set aside, covered with plastic wrap. Repeat with remaining wonton wrappers.

In a large wok, heat 4 cups (32 fl oz/1 L) vegetable oil until it reaches 375°F (190°C) on a deep-frying thermometer or until a small bread cube dropped in oil sizzles and turns golden. Working in batches, add wontons and fry until golden on both sides, 1–2 minutes. Using a slotted spoon, remove from wok and drain on paper towels. Serve wontons hot, accompanied with chili oil.

Tip

If round wonton wrappers are unavailable, purchase square wrappers and cut into rounds.

Ginger-sesame pork rolls

Makes 8 rolls

8 oz (250 g) ground (minced) pork

3 scallions (shallots/spring onions), finely chopped

2 tablespoons chopped canned bamboo shoots

1 teaspoon peeled and grated fresh ginger

¼ teaspoon five-spice powder

2 teaspoons soy sauce

1 teaspoon Asian sesame oil

8 bean curd sheets, 5 x 6 inches (13 x 15 cm)

¼ small red bell pepper (capsicum), seeded
   and thinly sliced

4 scallions (shallots/spring onions), green tops
   only, cut into 5-inch (13-cm) lengths

¼ cup (2 fl oz/60 ml) hoisin sauce

2 tablespoons shaoxing wine or dry sherry

2 teaspoons chopped fresh ginger

1 clove garlic, crushed

1 scallion (shallot/spring onion), finely chopped

In a bowl, combine pork, scallions, bamboo shoots, ginger, five-spice powder, soy sauce, and sesame oil. Mix well. Lightly brush bean curd sheets with cold water and lay flat on a work surface. Spread ⅛ of mixture along one end of each sheet. Lay strips of red bell pepper and scallions along meat and push gently until completely enclosed by meat. Fold two sides of sheet in and roll up, brushing remaining side lightly with water if needed. Press down firmly to seal.

Partially fill a large wok or pot with water (steamer should not touch water) and bring to a rapid simmer.

Line a bamboo steamer or steamer basket with parchment (baking) paper or leaves, leaving some space for steam to circulate efficiently. Arrange tofu rolls in a single layer in steamer. Place steamer over water, cover, and cook until pork mixture is firm and ready, about 10 minutes. Remove rolls from steamer.

For dipping sauce: In a bowl, combine hoisin sauce, wine, ginger, garlic and scallion. Mix well. Serve rolls whole or cut into diagonal pieces and stand with cut side up, with hoisin and ginger sauce for dipping.

Mini noodle baskets with crab and avocado

Makes 12

4 oz (125 g) fresh thin egg noodles
vegetable oil, for deep-frying
1 ripe avocado
juice of 1 lemon
4 oz (125 g) crabmeat, canned or fresh
4 oz (125 g) salmon roe

Soak noodles in boiling water for 10 minutes. Drain and pat dry with paper towels.

In a wok or frying pan, heat oil until it reaches 375°F (190°C) on a deep-frying thermometer or until a small bread cube dropped in oil sizzles and turns golden. Dip 2 strainers into oil to coat. Place 1 heaped tablespoon noodles in larger strainer. Press smaller strainer on top as firmly as possible. Plunge into oil and cook until golden and crisp, 1–2 minutes. Remove from oil. Lift basket from strainers and drain on paper towels. Repeat with remaining noodles. Set baskets aside and allow to cool. You should have 12 baskets.

Remove pit from avocado. Peel, cut into 12 thin slices and brush with lemon juice.

Place slice of avocado in each basket. Top with 1 teaspoon crabmeat and 1 teaspoon salmon roe. Serve immediately.

Tip

Noodle baskets not only look impressive but taste great. They can be made bite size or larger for serving individual portions. For this recipe, you can use a device specifically designed for making noodle nests and sold in Asian markets or specialty kitchen shops. Or you can use two heatproof strainers, one larger so that it holds the other. Be sure to dip the strainers in oil before putting the noodles in so they do not stick. The baskets can be made in advance of using and stored in an airtight container for up to five days.

Miso with scallops and ginger

Serves 4

8 oz (250 g) scallops, cut in half if large

¼ cup (1 oz/30 g) peeled and shredded
   fresh ginger

¼ cup (⅓ oz/10 g) chopped cilantro
   (fresh coriander)

1½ cups (12 fl oz/375 ml) water

1 lemongrass stalk, bruised and finely chopped

4 kaffir lime leaves, finely shredded,
   or 1 teaspoon grated lime zest (rind)

2 tablespoons red miso paste

1 teaspoon lime juice

In a wok, combine scallops, ginger, cilantro, water and lemongrass. Bring to a boil. Reduce heat, cover and simmer until scallops are opaque, 1–2 minutes.

Remove from heat and pour through strainer into bowl. Reserve liquid. Set scallops and spices aside and keep warm.

Measure liquid and add water to make 4 cups (32 fl oz/1 L). Return to wok and bring to a boil. Stir in miso and lime juice, reduce heat and simmer for 3 minutes.

To serve, divide scallops among individual plates. Ladle miso into small bowls.

Mixed vegetable pakoras

Makes about 28

2⅔ cups (14 oz/400 g) chickpea (garbanzo bean) flour

1 teaspoon whole ajwain seeds (see Tips below)

½ teaspoon chili powder

salt to taste

4 teaspoons vegetable oil

about 1¼ cups (10 fl oz/300 ml) water

vegetable oil for deep-frying

1 red bell pepper (capsicum), seeded and
    cut into ½-inch (12-mm) dice

1 medium desiree potato, peeled and
    cut into ½-inch (12-mm) dice

1 large red (Spanish) or yellow (brown) onion,
    cut into ½-inch (12-mm) dice

1 medium globe eggplant (aubergine), unpeeled,
    cut into ½-inch (12-mm) dice

mint raita (see page 228), for serving

In a bowl, combine flour, ajwain, chili powder and salt. In a small saucepan, heat oil until it begins to smoke, then quickly stir into flour mixture. Add enough water to form a thick smooth batter.

Fill a wok with vegetable oil to a depth of 3 inches (7.5 cm). Heat oil over medium–high heat to 375°F (190°C) on a deep-frying thermometer or until a small bread cube dropped in oil sizzles and turns golden. Meanwhile, add all diced vegetables to batter and mix well.

Working in batches of about seven pakoras, carefully drop 1 heaped tablespoon mixture for each pakora into hot oil. Cook, turning as necessary, until light golden brown, 1–2 minutes per side. Use a slotted spoon to remove pakoras to paper towels to drain. Repeat with remaining batter.

Just before serving pakoras, refry them in batches of seven, turning once, until crisp and golden brown, 1–2 minutes. Drain on paper towels. Serve immediately with mint raita.

Tips

- Ajwain seeds have the flavor of thyme with peppery overtones. Similar in appearance to celery seeds, they are used in Indian breads, fried snacks, and lentil and vegetable dishes.
- You can do the initial frying of pakoras up to 6 hours ahead. Instead of dicing vegetables, you can cut them into thin slices, dip them in batter, then deep-fry slices until golden brown.

Peanut and chili bundles

Serves 8–10 as appetizer, 6 as entrée

1 cup (5½ oz/165 g) unsalted roasted peanuts
1 small red chili, seeded and finely chopped
8 scallions (shallots/green onions), finely chopped
¼ cup (⅓ oz/10 g) chopped cilantro (fresh coriander)
½ cup (4 fl oz/125 ml) lemon juice
½ cup (1 oz/30 g) fresh white bread crumbs
1 teaspoon superfine (caster) sugar
24 wonton wrappers
4 cups (32 fl oz/1 L) vegetable oil, for deep-frying
lime wedges and sweet chili sauce or soy
    sauce, for serving

In a food processor or blender, process peanuts until fine.
Transfer to bowl. Add chili, scallions, cilantro, lemon juice,
bread crumbs and sugar. Mix well.

Place wonton wrappers on work surface and cover with
damp towel to prevent them from drying out. Working with
one wrapper at a time, place 1 teaspoon peanut filling in
middle. Brush edges with water, gather edges together and
twist to seal. Set aside, covered with plastic wrap. Repeat
with remaining wonton wrappers.

In a wok, heat oil until it reaches 375°F (190°C) on a deep-
frying thermometer or until a small bread cube dropped in
oil sizzles and turns golden. Working in batches, add
wontons and fry until golden, 1–2 minutes. Using slotted
spoon, remove from wok and drain on paper towels.

Serve bundles hot with lime wedges and with sweet chili
sauce or soy sauce for dipping.

Portuguese-style shrimp

Serves 4–6

Reichado masala
4 dried red chilies, broken into small pieces
4 teaspoons black peppercorns
1 teaspoon cumin seeds
¼ cup (2 fl oz/60 ml) white vinegar
4 teaspoons crushed garlic
1½ teaspoons tamarind concentrate
½ teaspoon ground turmeric

**2 lb (1 kg) medium shrimp (prawns), peeled
  and deveined**
2 tablespoons vegetable oil
juice of 1 lemon

For reichado masala: In a spice grinder, grind chilies, peppercorns and cumin seeds (without roasting) to a powder. In a small bowl, combine vinegar, garlic and tamarind. Stir in ground spices and turmeric, and mix well. Set aside to stand for 10–20 minutes before using.

In a glass or ceramic bowl, combine reichado masala and shrimp and mix well to coat shrimp. Set aside to marinate for 5 minutes.

In a wok, heat oil over medium–low heat until hot. Cook shrimp in batches, turning once, until browned, about 1–2 minutes. Take care not to scorch marinade. Drizzle cooked shrimp with lemon juice and serve hot.

Tips

- Reichado masala can be kept in an airtight jar and stored in refrigerator for up to 6 months.
- As a variation, lightly brush shrimp with reichado masala. Cook shrimp in batches as above and set aside. In a small saucepan, heat 2 tablespoons vegetable oil over medium–high heat. Cook 20 curry leaves—or as many as desired—until fragrant, about 30 seconds. Drain on paper towels and toss with shrimp. If desired, add thinly sliced red (Spanish) onion for color.

Pot stickers

Serves 4

8 oz (250 g) ground (minced) lean pork
1 onion, finely chopped
1 cup (3 oz/90 g) finely shredded green cabbage
2 teaspoons peeled and grated fresh ginger
1 tablespoon Asian sesame oil
1 tablespoon soy sauce
1 teaspoon white pepper
24 round wheat wonton wrappers
4 tablespoons vegetable oil
2 cups (16 fl oz/500 ml) chicken stock (see page 220),
    or as needed
light soy sauce, for serving

In a bowl, combine pork, onion, cabbage, ginger, sesame oil, soy sauce and pepper. Mix well.

Place wonton wrappers on work surface and cover with damp kitchen towel to prevent them from drying out. Working with one wrapper at a time, lay it on work surface and place 1 teaspoon filling in middle. Brush edges with water, fold wonton in half and press edges together to seal. Using your fingertips, pinch frill around each folded wonton if desired. Set aside, covered with plastic wrap. Repeat with remaining wrappers.

In a heavy-bottomed pan over medium–high heat, heat 1 tablespoon vegetable oil. Swirl to cover entire bottom of pan. Working in batches, fry filled wontons until golden brown on both sides, about 1 minute. Coat pan as needed with remaining 3 tablespoons vegetable oil.

Return pot stickers to pan and add enough stock to come halfway up sides of pot stickers. Cover and simmer until stock is almost absorbed, about 10 minutes. Uncover and cook until stock is completely absorbed and bottoms of pot stickers are crisp. Repeat with remaining pot stickers. Serve pot stickers warm with soy sauce.

Tip

These panfried pork dumplings originally got their name because they tend to stick to the pot during cooking. Though messy, the dumplings have an authentic flavor and appearance.

Rice flour crisps

Serves 4

1½ cups (12 oz/375 g) rice flour

⅓ cup (2 oz/ 60 g) besan flour

1 tablespoon cumin seeds

1 teaspoon chili powder

1 teaspoon ground coriander

2 tablespoons ghee

about 1 cup (8 fl oz/250 ml) coconut milk

3 cups (24 fl oz/750 ml) vegetable oil, for deep-frying

2 teaspoons sea salt

Sift flours into a bowl. Add cumin seeds, chili powder and coriander. Rub ghee into dry ingredients, using your fingers. Make a well in the center and stir in enough coconut milk to make a soft batter. Spoon batter into a piping bag fitted with a ½-inch (12-mm) star tip.

In a large wok, heat oil until it reaches 375°F (190°C) on a deep-frying thermometer or until a small bread cube dropped in oil sizzles and turns golden. Working in batches, carefully pipe 2-inch (5-cm) lengths of batter into hot oil and fry until golden and crisp, about 1 minute. Using a slotted spoon, transfer to paper towels to drain. Sprinkle with salt and serve immediately.

Savory rice bites

Makes 16–20 squares

1½ tablespoons tamarind pulp
½ cup (4 fl oz/125 ml) boiling water
1 cup (7 oz/220 g) white glutinous rice
2 teaspoons grated fresh turmeric
1 teaspoon finely peeled and grated fresh ginger
¾ cup (6 fl oz/180 ml) thin coconut cream or
    coconut milk
2 scallions (shallots/spring onions), finely chopped
¼ cup (⅓ oz/10 g) cilantro (fresh coriander) leaves,
    finely chopped
3 kaffir lime leaves, spines removed, finely chopped
¼ teaspoon grated kaffir lime zest (rind)
1 red chili, seeded and finely chopped (optional)
6 oz (185 g) barbecued pork (available from Asian
    food stores) or barbecued chicken, sliced
Sweet chili, satay, or hoisin sauce, for serving

Place tamarind pulp in a small bowl and cover with boiling water. Mix well, breaking up pulp with a spoon to release flavor. Let stand for 5 minutes, then push through a fine-meshed strainer, discarding pulp and reserving liquid.

Wrap turmeric in a cheesecloth (muslin) square and tie with string. Put rice, turmeric and tamarind liquid in a medium bowl. Cover with cold water and let soak overnight. Drain, removing turmeric. Line a bamboo steamer or steamer basket with cheese-cloth (muslin) and spread rice evenly on top.

Partially fill a wok or pot with water (steamer should not touch water) and bring to a rapid simmer.

Place steamer over water, cover, and steam until rice is just tender, 30–35 minutes, adding more water to wok if required. Remove steamer from heat and put rice in a bowl.

Gently fold in ginger, coconut cream, scallions, cilantro, lime leaves, lime zest and chili. Spread rice evenly in an 8-inch (20-cm) square baking pan lined with parchment (baking) paper and refrigerate until set, about 2 hours. Cut into 16–20 squares to serve. Top with a small piece of barbecued pork or chicken and a dash of sweet chili, satay or hoisin sauce.

Shrimp and coconut fritters

Serves 6–8

10 oz (300 g) small raw shrimp (prawns), coarsely chopped

2 cups (16 fl oz/500 ml) water

1 cup (5 oz/150 g) self-raising flour

⅓ cup (1 oz/30 g) unsweetened dried (desiccated) shredded coconut

½ teaspoon baking powder

1 teaspoon salt

1 large egg

⅓ teaspoon black pepper

2 scallions (shallots/spring onions), finely chopped

1 small clove garlic, finely chopped

2 teaspoons fresh dill or cilantro (fresh coriander), chopped

2 tablespoons vegetable oil

sweet chili sauce, for serving

Peel the shrimp and place shells in a saucepan with water. Bring to a boil, simmer for 10 minutes, then strain liquid into a pitcher and let cool.

In a bowl, combine shrimp and remaining ingredients, except oil and chili sauce. Slowly add cooled, reserved liquid to make a creamy batter, adding extra cold water if necessary. Set aside for 25 minutes.

In a wok, heat oil over medium heat. Add large tablespoonfuls of batter and cook until golden brown underneath, then turn and cook other side. The fritters are done when they feel firm in the middle and no uncooked batter exudes when pressed. Remove from wok using a slotted spoon and drain on paper towels. Keep warm until remainder are cooked. Serve immediately with sweet chili sauce.

Shrimp and lemongrass sticks

Makes 12

1½ lb (750 g) jumbo shrimp (green king prawns),
  peeled and deveined
3 cloves garlic, chopped
2 teaspoons peeled and grated fresh ginger
6 scallions (shallots/spring onions), chopped
¼ cup (⅓ oz/10 g) chopped cilantro
  (fresh coriander)
1 teaspoon sambal oelek (see page 230)
3 teaspoons fish sauce
2 tablespoons cornstarch (cornflour)
6 lemongrass stalks, trimmed and cut into 12 pieces
  about 4 inches (10 cm) long
¼ cup (1 oz/30 g) cornstarch (cornflour), for dusting
3 cups (24 fl oz/750 ml) vegetable oil, for frying
soy sauce or chili oil (see page 223), for dipping

In a food processor, process shrimp until a thick paste forms, about 20 seconds. Add garlic, ginger, scallions, cilantro, sambal oelek, fish sauce and 2 tablespoons cornstarch and process until well combined, about 10 seconds. Using wet hands, divide mixture into 12 portions. Mold each portion around end of a lemongrass piece. Lightly dust with cornstarch, shaking off any excess.

In a large wok, heat oil until it reaches 375°F (190°C) on a deep-frying thermometer or until a small bread cube dropped in oil sizzles and turns golden. Working in batches, add lemongrass sticks and cook until golden, 3–4 minutes. Using a slotted spoon, remove from hot oil and drain on paper towels. Serve hot with soy sauce or chili oil for dipping.

Sweet corn fritters

Serves 4–5

1 lb (500 g) potatoes, peeled and cubed
1 egg, beaten
¼ cup (2 fl oz/60 ml) cream
¼ cup (1½ oz/45 g) all-purpose (plain) flour
kernels from 2 corn cobs, about 2 cups (12 oz/375 g)
¼ cup (¼ oz/7 g) cilantro (fresh coriander) leaves,
   finely chopped
1 egg white
sea salt and freshly ground black pepper to taste
3 tablespoons vegetable oil
⅓ cup (3 fl oz/90 ml) sweet chili sauce, for dipping

Preheat oven to 225°F (110°C/Gas ¼). Bring a saucepan of salted water to a boil. Add potatoes and cook until soft but not mushy, 6–8 minutes. Drain well, place in a bowl and mash with a fork or potato masher. Allow to cool slightly. Add egg and cream and mix well. Stir in flour, corn and cilantro.

In a bowl, using a balloon whisk or electric beater, beat egg white until soft peaks form. Gently fold egg white into corn mixture and season with salt and pepper.

In a heavy-bottomed wok, warm oil over medium heat. For each fritter, spoon 2 tablespoons corn mixture into hot pan. Cook fritters until golden, 2–3 minutes per side. Remove from pan and drain on paper towels. Keep warm in oven. Serve with sweet chili sauce for dipping.

Vegetarian spring rolls

Makes 18–20

4 Chinese dried mushrooms
2 oz (60 g) cellophane (bean thread) noodles
   or rice vermicelli
2 tablespoons vegetable oil
1 onion, finely chopped
2 cloves garlic, chopped
2 tablespoons peeled and grated fresh ginger
2 cups (6 oz/180 g) shredded green cabbage
2 carrots, peeled and grated
⅓ cup (½ oz/15 g) chopped cilantro
   (fresh coriander)
1 cup (4 oz/125 g) fresh bean sprouts, rinsed
2 teaspoons fish sauce
2 teaspoons cornstarch (cornflour) mixed
   in 2 tablespoons water
18–20 frozen spring roll wrappers, thawed
vegetable oil, for deep-frying
sweet chili sauce, for serving

Place mushrooms in a small bowl, add boiling water to cover and let stand for 10–15 minutes. Drain and squeeze out excess liquid. Thinly slice mushrooms, discarding tough stems.

Soak noodles in boiling water for 10 minutes. Drain and roughly chop into short lengths.

In a wok or frying pan over medium–high heat, warm 2 tablespoons oil. Add onion, garlic and ginger and cook until softened, about 2 minutes. Add cabbage and stir-fry until cabbage is softened, 1–2 minutes. Remove from heat and stir in carrots, cilantro, bean sprouts, noodles, mushrooms and fish sauce. Mix well and cool completely.

Separate spring roll wrappers, place on a work surface and cover with damp kitchen towel to prevent them from drying out. Working with one wrapper at a time, place on work surface. Using your fingertips, wet edges with cornstarch and water mixture. Place 1 heaped tablespoon filling in middle of wrapper. Roll up diagonally, tucking in edges. Seal edge with cornstarch and water mixture. Repeat with remaining wrappers.

In a wok or frying pan, heat oil until it reaches 375°F (190°C) on a deep-frying thermometer or until a small bread cube dropped in oil sizzles and turns golden. Working in batches, add rolls and fry until golden, 1–2 minutes. Using a slotted spoon, remove from pan and drain on paper towels. Serve hot, accompanied with chili sauce.

chicken and duck

Braised duck with pineapple

Serves 4

1 duck (about 3 lb/1.5 kg) or duck pieces
(see Tips opposite)

½ cup (2 oz/60 g) finely chopped brown or pink
shallots (French shallots)

6 cloves garlic, finely chopped

about ½ teaspoon ground pepper

2 tablespoons fish sauce

2–3 tablespoons vegetable oil

3 cups (24 fl oz/750 ml) chicken stock (see page 220)

2 tablespoons distilled rice alcohol or vodka

1 fresh pineapple, peeled, or one 28-oz (850-g)
can pineapple rings, drained

1 tablespoon sugar

1 teaspoon salt or to taste

1 tablespoon arrowroot or cornstarch (cornflour)
mixed with 1 tablespoon water

cilantro (fresh coriander) sprigs, for garnish

coarsely ground pepper to taste

If using whole duck, begin by placing duck on a cutting board. Pull each leg away from body and use a cleaver or large chef's knife to cut through the joint attaching it to the body. Likewise, pull each wing away from body and cut through its joint. Cut duck carcass in half lengthwise by cutting through bones connecting breast and back. Remove and discard any large bones as necessary. Now cut down along backbone, turn over duck, and cut lengthwise through breastbone. You should have 8 pieces. Cut each section crosswise through the bones into bite-sized pieces.

In a large bowl, toss duck pieces with shallots, garlic, pepper and fish sauce. Let stand at room temperature for 1 hour or refrigerate overnight. Using a slotted spoon, transfer duck to a plate, reserving marinade. Pat duck dry with paper towels.

In a large wok or frying pan, heat oil over medium heat. Add duck pieces, skin-side down, and cook until golden brown and all fat has been extracted, about 15–20 minutes. Drain off and discard fat. For a lighter, skin-free version, refer to the Tip opposite.

Transfer duck to a heavy pot. Add stock, liquor and reserved marinade. Bring to a very gentle boil, then immediately reduce heat to low, cover, and cook at a bare simmer until tender, about 20 minutes.

Meanwhile, cut fresh pineapple in half lengthwise, then into half-moons ½ inch (12 mm) thick. Use a small paring knife to remove core. Alternatively, cut canned pineapple rings in half crosswise. In a large, nonstick wok over medium heat, lightly brown pineapple pieces, sprinkling with sugar to create a light caramel glaze. Alternatively, use a large wok oiled with 1 tablespoon vegetable oil or butter, or vegetable oil cooking spray. Remove from heat and set aside.

When duck is almost done, add pineapple and taste for seasoning, adding salt to taste. Cook for a few minutes for flavors to meld. Using a slotted spoon, transfer duck and pineapple to a bowl; cover to keep warm. Strain cooking liquid. If liquid appears greasy, lightly float paper towels on the surface to absorb fat.

Add arrowroot mixture to sauce. Bring to a boil, stirring. Spoon some of this sauce over duck pieces. Serve additional sauce alongside. Garnish with cilantro sprigs and, sprinkle with coarsely ground pepper.

Tips

- For a lighter version, use skinless duck pieces. Fry duck pieces until lightly browned, for only 2–3 minutes. Likewise, boneless, skinless duck breast can be used; simmer until just tender, 10–15 minutes.
- For braised duck with orange, substitute an equal quantity of peeled orange segments for pineapple.

Chicken and cashew stir-fry

Serves 4

2 tablespoons vegetable oil

4 oz (100 g) cashew nut kernels

1 bunch scallions (shallots/spring onions), trimmed
and sliced

4–5 sticks celery, thinly sliced

4 chicken breasts, skinned and cut in ½-inch (1.5-cm)
cubes

6 oz (150 g) stir-fry yellow bean sauce

salt and pepper

steamed rice, for serving

In a wok or a heavy-based saucepan or skillet, add the oil and heat it until it smokes. Toss in the cashew nuts, onions and celery and cook for 1–2 minutes, stirring frequently over a fairly fierce heat until the nuts are lightly browned. Add the chicken and cook quickly, stirring frequently for 2–3 minutes until sealed and just cooked. Add the yellow bean sauce, season lightly and cook for a further minutes or so until piping hot.

Serve at once with steamed rice.

Chicken chow mein

Serves 4

6 cups (48 fl oz/1.5 L) vegetable oil, for deep-frying,
   plus 2 tablespoons oil

6½ oz (200 g) fresh thin egg noodles

3 cloves garlic, crushed

1 tablespoon peeled and grated fresh ginger

1 onion, cut into eighths

1 lb (500 g) skinless chicken thigh fillets, cut
   into ¾-inch (2-cm) cubes

1 red bell pepper (capsicum), seeded and sliced

1 green bell pepper (capsicum), seeded and sliced

1 bunch choy sum or spinach, trimmed and
   cut into 2-inch (5-cm) lengths

3 tablespoons hoisin sauce

¼ cup (2 fl oz/60 ml) chicken stock (see page 220)
   mixed with 1 teaspoon cornstarch (cornflour)

In a wok, heat 6 cups (48 fl oz/1.5 L) oil until it reaches 375°F (190°C) on a deep-frying thermometer or until a small bread cube dropped in oil sizzles and turns golden. Working in small batches, add noodles and fry until golden and crisp, 1–2 minutes. Using slotted spoon, remove from oil and drain on paper towels.

In a wok over medium-high heat, warm 2 tablespoons vegetable oil. Add garlic, ginger and onion and stir-fry until onion softens slightly, about 3 minutes. Add chicken and stir-fry until browned, 3–4 minutes. Add bell peppers and choy sum or spinach and stir-fry until tender-crisp, about 2 minutes. Stir in hoisin sauce and stock and cornstarch mixture and cook until sauce boils and thickens slightly, about 2 minutes.

To serve, arrange crisp noodles in nest on serving plates. Top with chicken and vegetables.

Chicken satay salad

Serves 4

1 cup (8 fl oz/250 ml) coconut milk

½ cup (5 oz/155 g) crunchy peanut butter

1 tablespoon fish sauce

1 tablespoon soy sauce

1 tablespoon peeled and grated fresh ginger

1 tablespoon palm sugar or brown sugar

1 teaspoon red chili flakes

6½ oz (200 g) rice stick noodles

4 cloves garlic, crushed

3 tablespoons fish sauce

1 tablespoon soy sauce

1 tablespoon minced lemongrass or 2 teaspoons
     grated lemon zest (rind)

1 lb (500 g) skinless chicken breast fillets, sliced

2 tablespoons vegetable oil

3 carrots, peeled and julienned

1 cup (4 oz/125 g) fresh bean sprouts, rinsed

¼ cup (⅓ oz/10 g) chopped cilantro (fresh coriander)

1 bunch mizuna or 1 head butter lettuce, leaves
     separated and trimmed

lime wedges for serving

In a food processor, combine coconut milk, peanut butter, fish and soy sauces, ginger, sugar and red chili flakes. Process 10 seconds. Transfer to bowl and set aside.

Cook noodles, then drain and allow to cool. In a glass or ceramic bowl, combine garlic, fish and soy sauces and lemongrass or zest. Add chicken and turn to coat in marinade. Cover and allow to marinate in refrigerator 1 hour. Drain.

In a wok, heat oil over medium-high heat. Add chicken and cook, stirring, until golden and tender, 4–5 minutes. Add to satay sauce and toss.

In bowl, combine carrots, bean sprouts, noodles and cilantro.

To serve, arrange mizuna or lettuce leaves on individual plates. Top with vegetable-noodle mixture. Spoon on chicken and sauce. Serve warm or chilled with lime wedges.

Chicken stir-fry with bean sprouts

Serves 4

4 boneless chicken breasts, skinned
salt and pepper
3 tablespoons oil, preferably sesame or walnut
1 clove garlic, crushed
6 oz (185 g) carrots, peeled and cut into thin sticks
2 cups (8 oz/250 g) fresh bean sprouts
3–4 oz (90–125 g) snow peas (mange-tout), trimmed
7-oz (220-g) can pineapple pieces in natural juice
2 tablespoons light soy sauce
1 tablespoon sesame seeds
steamed rice, for serving

Cut chicken into strips and season lightly with salt and pepper.

In a wok or large heavy-based pan, heat 2 tablespoons oil and stir-fry chicken pieces briskly until browned and cooked through. Remove from wok and set aside.

Add remaining oil, garlic and carrots to wok and stir-fry for 3–4 minutes, stirring constantly. Add bean sprouts and snow peas and cook for 2–3 minutes, stirring.

Drain pineapple, reserving 2 tablespoons juice. Add pineapple to wok with cooked chicken, reserved pineapple juice and soy sauce, and season to taste. Heat through thoroughly. Sprinkle with sesame seeds.

Serve immediately with steamed rice.

Chicken with ginger

Serves 4–6

1 cup (2 oz/60 g) cloud or tree ear mushrooms
   (black or white fungus)

¼ cup (2 fl oz/60 ml) vegetable oil

6 cloves garlic, coarsely chopped

1 small onion, thinly sliced

12 oz (375 g) boneless, skinless chicken breasts,
   thinly sliced

1 cup (4 oz/125 g) loosely packed, julienned fresh
   ginger, preferably young ginger

1 tablespoon fish sauce

3 tablespoons oyster sauce

1 tablespoon soy sauce

1 tablespoon soybean paste

2 fresh long red chilies, cut into large pieces

½ cup (4 fl oz/125 ml) chicken stock (see page 220)

8 scallions (shallots/spring onions), white part only,
   chopped

If using dried mushrooms, soak in water for 10 minutes;
drain. Use scissors to trim hard core, then cut mushrooms
into pieces.

In a wok or large, heavy frying pan, heat oil over high heat
and fry garlic just until it starts to brown. Immediately add
onion and chicken, and stir-fry until meat is opaque on all
sides, about 2 minutes.

Add ginger and mushrooms, then fish sauce, oyster sauce,
soy sauce, and soybean paste. Stir-fry for 1 minute. Add
chilies and stock or water, bring to a boil, and cook for
1 minute. Stir in scallions. Transfer to a serving dish and
serve.

Tip

If cloud or tree ear mushrooms are unavailable, use an equal
quantity of straw mushrooms or standard mushrooms.

Chicken with lemongrass and chili

Serves 6

1½ lb (750 g) chicken (thigh portions)
1 tablespoon fish sauce
salt and black pepper to taste
2 lemongrass stalks, trimmed
2 scallions (shallots/spring onions), trimmed
3 tablespoons vegetable oil
1 cup (8 fl oz/250 ml) water
2 fresh red chilies, seeded and sliced
1 teaspoon crumbled palm or brown sugar
steamed rice, for serving

Cut chicken portions in half, through bone. Using a sharp skewer, prick chicken. Place chicken in a dish and pour over fish sauce, sprinkle on salt and pepper and let stand for 15 minutes.

Very finely chop lemongrass and scallions. In a wok, heat oil and brown chicken evenly. Add lemongrass and scallions and water. Cover and cook until chicken is almost tender, about 15 minutes, turning several times. Add chilies and sugar and cook for a further 5–7 minutes. The liquid should evaporate, leaving chicken free of sauce. Serve immediately with steamed rice.

Chili chicken and vegetables

Serves 4

2 tablespoons peanut oil

1 small red chili, seeded and
finely chopped

5 oz (150 g) skinless chicken breast or thigh
fillet, cut into 1-inch (2.5-cm) cubes

6 asparagus spears, cut into 1¼-inch (3-cm) pieces

1 bunch bok choy, trimmed and large leaves halved

4 oz (125 g) sugar snap peas or snow peas
(mange-touts), trimmed

4 oz (125 g) shiitake mushrooms, sliced

¼ cup (2 fl oz/60 ml) chicken stock (see page 220)

2 teaspoons soy sauce

1 tablespoon rice wine

1 teaspoon Asian sesame oil

crisp fried egg noodles for serving (optional)

In a wok over medium heat, warm peanut oil. Add chili and chicken and stir-fry until chicken is golden, 4–5 minutes. Raise heat to medium–high, add asparagus, bok choy sugar snap peas or snow peas and mushrooms and stir-fry until vegetables soften slightly, 3–4 minutes.

In a small bowl, combine stock, soy sauce, rice wine and sesame oil. Add to wok, reduce heat to medium and cook until heated through.

Serve hot, with crisp fried egg noodles if desired.

Crispy wontons with duck

Serves 4

10 scallions (shallots/spring onions), pale portion
    only, cut into 2-inch (5-cm) pieces
2 carrots, peeled and julienned
1 Chinese roasted duck
6 cups (48 fl oz/1.5 L) vegetable oil, for deep-frying
16 wonton wrappers
½ cup (4 fl oz/125 ml) hoisin sauce

Using sharp knife or scissors, make ¼-inch (6-mm) cuts
into ends of each scallion piece to make fringe. Place
scallions and carrots in bowl of ice water. Refrigerate until
scallions curl, about 15 minutes.

Remove meat and skin from duck and coarsely chop;
discard skin if desired. In a wok, heat oil until it reaches
375°F (190°C) on a deep-frying thermometer or until a small
bread cube dropped in oil sizzles and turns golden. Working
with one wonton at a time and using two sets of tongs,
hold wonton in taco shape and lower into oil. Continue to
hold wonton until golden and crisp, about 1 minute. Drain
on paper towels. Repeat with remaining wontons.

To serve, fill wontons with scallions, carrots and duck.
Drizzle with hoisin sauce and serve immediately.

Duck with long beans

Serves 4

1 Chinese roasted duck

2 teaspoons vegetable oil

4 scallions (shallots/spring onions), chopped

1 tablespoon peeled and shredded fresh ginger

8 long beans, cut into 2½-inch (6-cm) lengths

2 tablespoons shredded orange zest (rind)

2 tablespoons mirin

1½ tablespoons light soy sauce

steamed white rice, for serving

Cut duck into serving pieces, leaving flesh on bone. Set aside. In a wok over medium–high heat, warm vegetable oil. Add scallions and ginger and stir-fry until softened, about 2 minutes. Add beans, orange zest, duck, mirin and soy sauce and stir-fry until heated through, 3–4 minutes.

Serve hot, accompanied with steamed white rice.

Green chicken curry

Serves 4–6

2 tablespoon vegetable oil

1 onion, chopped

1 tablespoon green curry paste or to taste

1 lb (500 g) skinless chicken thigh fillets, cut
   into thin strips

5 oz (150 g) green beans, trimmed

1¾ cups (14 fl oz/440 ml) coconut milk

4 kaffir lime leaves

1 tablespoon fish sauce

1 teaspoon grated lime zest (rind)

1 tablespoon lime juice

1 tablespoon brown sugar

2 tablespoons chopped cilantro (fresh coriander)

steamed white rice, for serving

In a wok over medium heat, warm vegetable oil. Add onion and curry paste and stir-fry until onion softens, 1–2 minutes. Add chicken and stir-fry until lightly golden, 3–4 minutes. Add beans, coconut milk and lime leaves and bring to a boil. Reduce heat to low and simmer, uncovered, until beans are tender-crisp, 3–4 minutes. Add fish sauce, lime zest and juice, sugar and cilantro. Cook for 1 minute.

Serve hot, accompanied with steamed white rice.

Grilled chicken drumsticks

Serves 4

5 chicken drumsticks
1 tablespoon ginger juice (obtained by grating
   fresh ginger)
1 tablespoon vegetable or sunflower oil
2 tablespoons light soy sauce
1 tablespoon sugar
1 tablespoon malt liquid (mullyeot)
1 tablespoon rice wine
1 tablespoon chopped parsley, for garnish

Score drumsticks all over with tip of a knife to allow ginger flavor to penetrate. Place drumsticks in a medium bowl and drizzle with ginger juice. Marinate for 15 minutes, turning frequently to coat with juice.

In a wok over medium heat, heat 1 tablespoon of oil. Add drumsticks and fry until golden, about 5 minutes. Remove and keep warm. Keep sauce in pan.

Add soy sauce, sugar, malt liquid and rice wine to pan juices. Boil over high heat until liquid is reduced by half, about 5 minutes.

Using a brush, coat drumsticks with the sauce. Return to wok and cook over high heat until sauce caramelizes and chicken is cooked, 5–8 minutes. Test with a skewer; chicken is done when juices run clear.

Transfer drumsticks to a serving plate and wrap the bone ends in foil. Garnish with parsley and serve as finger food with steamed rice.

Tip
Malt liquid has a slightly sweet flavor. It is added to dishes for presentation as it adds a shine.

Indonesian-style chicken fried rice

Serves 4

2 cups (12 oz/375 g) long-grain rice

1 tablespoon vegetable oil

1 tablespoon Asian sesame oil

1 lb (500 g) chicken breast fillet, chopped

1 carrot, sliced into thin strips

1 medium-size green bell pepper (capsicum),
  seeded and thinly sliced

1 teaspoon Chinese five-spice powder

1 teaspoon ground coriander

½ teaspoon ground cumin

1 tablespoon finely grated fresh ginger

2 cloves garlic, minced

1 small chili, finely chopped

¼ cup (2 fl oz/60 ml) soy sauce

8 oz (250 g) bean sprouts

6 scallions (shallots/spring onions), sliced

Cook the rice according to package instructions. Drain, then return to pan, cover tightly with lid and set aside.

In a wok or large frying pan, heat the vegetable and sesame oil. Add chicken and stir-fry until lightly browned and tender, about 4 minutes. Add carrot and bell pepper and continue stir-frying for 2 minutes. Stir in spices.

Stir rice with fork and add to wok with remaining ingredients. Cook, stirring, 3 minutes to mix and heat through.

Larb salad with chicken

Serves 4–6

2 tablespoons sticky (glutinous) rice

2 thin slices fresh galangal

12 oz (375 g) boneless, skinless chicken
    breasts, ground (minced)

2 tablespoons thinly sliced shallots (French
    shallots), preferably pink

3 tablespoons fish sauce

2 tablespoons fresh lime juice

2–3 teaspoons chili powder, to taste

1 tablespoon coarsely chopped cilantro (fresh
    coriander) leaves and stems

1 scallion (shallot/spring onion), including green part,
    coarsely chopped

1 tablespoon coarsely chopped fresh mint

In a wok or small frying pan over low-medium heat, stir rice until golden brown, 3–5 minutes. Transfer to a mortar and pound to a coarse powder with a pestle. Transfer to a bowl and set aside. Pound galangal in the mortar until pulverized.

In a medium bowl, combine ground chicken, galangal, shallots, fish sauce, lime juice, and chili powder to taste; mix thoroughly. Heat a wok or large, heavy frying pan over medium heat and add chicken mixture all at once, stirring vigorously to keep it from sticking into lumps. Cook until opaque throughout, about 5 minutes.

Transfer to a bowl, and let cool slightly, then toss with ground rice and all remaining ingredients. If desired, garnish with additional mint leaves, and accompany with vegetable crudités, such as cabbage, carrot, cucumber, and long beans.

Tips

- Ask your butcher to grind the chicken, or do it yourself in a food processor.
- For Larb with Pork: Substitute an equal quantity ground pork for chicken, and cook as above.

Orange rice with chicken

Serves 5–6

2 oranges
2 cups (16 fl oz/500 ml) water
1 cup (8 oz/250 g) white sugar
4 tablespoons ghee or oil
½ cup (2 oz/60 g) slivered blanched almonds
2 lb (1 kg) boneless chicken breasts, quartered
1 tablespoon salt, plus extra salt to taste
freshly ground black pepper
1 medium-sized yellow (brown) onion, sliced
2 cups (14 oz/440 g) basmati rice
½ cup (1 oz/30 g) shelled, blanched pistachio nuts,
 chopped
½ teaspoon saffron threads, steeped in 2 tablespoons
 hot water for 10 minutes

Remove zest (rind) from oranges with vegetable peeler and cut into fine shreds about 1¼ inches (3 cm) long. In a small saucepan, bring water to a boil. Add zest and boil for 5 minutes. Drain and rinse.

Place 1 cup (8 fl oz/250 ml) water in same saucepan. Add sugar and orange zest, bring to a boil, reduce heat to medium–low and boil until syrup is thick, about 10 minutes. Set aside.

In a wok over medium–low heat, heat 1 tablespoon ghee or oil. Add almonds and fry gently until golden. Remove from pan and set aside. Heat remaining ghee or oil in the wok, add chicken and brown. Move chicken to a plate, leaving fat in wok, and season with salt and pepper. Add onion to the wok and fry gently over medium–low heat until soft and slightly browned, about 10 minutes. Add 1 cup (8 fl oz/250 ml) water and stir to deglaze wok. Add chicken, cover and simmer for 10 minutes.

In a large pot, bring 8 cups (64 fl oz/2 L) water to a boil. Add rice and 1 tablespoon salt. Return to boil and cook for 8 minutes. Drain rice in a sieve or colander and turn into a bowl. Strain syrup from orange over rice, reserving zest.

Preheat oven to 300°F (150°C/Gas 2). Butter a large baking dish (casserole) and spread half of the rice in it. Arrange chicken pieces and onion on top of rice. Add half the cooking liquid from chicken. Sprinkle with half the orange zest and almonds. Spread remaining rice on top, pour remaining chicken cooking liquid evenly over top, cover and bake for 40 minutes. Remove top layer of rice from dish and arrange around the edge of a warm serving platter. Remove chicken to a plate and place remaining rice in center of platter. Top with chicken pieces and garnish with remaining orange zest and almonds. Sprinkle with pistachio nuts. Pour saffron liquid over the rice around chicken.

Peking duck pancakes

Makes 15

Pancakes

¾ cup (4 oz/125 g) all-purpose (plain) flour

⅓ cup (1½ oz/45 g) cornstarch (cornflour)

2 eggs, beaten

¾ cup (6 fl oz/180 ml) water

¼ cup (2 fl oz/60 ml) milk

2 teaspoons superfine (caster) sugar

1 tablespoon vegetable oil

Filling

15 scallions (shallots/spring onions)

2 carrots, peeled and cut into thin sticks

1 Chinese roasted duck

¼ cup (2 fl oz/60 ml) hoisin sauce

1 tablespoon rice wine

15 chives

⅓ cup (3 fl oz/90 ml) hoisin sauce, for dipping

To make pancakes: Sift flour and cornstarch into a bowl. In a separate bowl, whisk together eggs, water, milk and sugar. Make a well in center of dry ingredients, gradually add egg mixture and beat until smooth.

In a frying pan, heat oil over medium heat, pour in 2 tablespoons of pancake batter and swirl pan gently to form a round pancake. Cook until golden, about 2 minutes. Turn and cook other side for 10 seconds. Remove from pan and repeat with remaining batter and oil.

To make filling: Cut into each end of scallions with a sharp knife or scissors to form a fringe. Place scallions and carrots in a bowl of iced water and refrigerate for 15 minutes, or until scallions curl. Remove meat and skin from duck and roughly chop. Combine hoisin sauce and rice wine.

Lay pancakes on work surface and place 1 tablespoon of duck meat and skin in center of each one. Top with 1 teaspoon of hoisin and rice wine mixture. Add a scallion curl and 3–4 carrot sticks. Roll and secure with a chive, trimming off any excess chive. Serve with hoisin sauce for dipping.

Red curry with roasted duck

Serves 4–6

2 cups (16 fl oz/500 ml) coconut milk

2–3 tablespoons vegetable oil (optional)

3 tablespoons fresh or commercial red curry paste
  (see page 231)

3 kaffir limes leaves, stemmed

12 oz (375 g) roasted, boneless duck meat

1 cup (1 oz/30 g) loosely packed fresh sweet
  Thai basil leaves

½ cup (2 oz/40 g) fresh green peppercorns on
  the stem, or 2–4 tablespoons canned green
  peppercorns, drained

1 cup (4 oz/125 g) eggplant (aubergine) cut into
  ½-inch (12-mm) pieces or 4 round Thai eggplants

½ cup (2 oz/60 g) pea eggplants (optional)

1 cup (6 oz/185 g) fresh or canned pineapple
  chunks, drained

6 cherry tomatoes

10 grapes

1 fresh long red chili, coarsely chopped

2 tablespoons fish sauce

2 tablespoons soy sauce

1 tablespoon granulated (white) sugar

1 tablespoon palm sugar

Let coconut milk stand, allowing the thick coconut milk to rise to the top. Spoon thick coconut milk into a small bowl, reserving 2 tablespoons for garnish.

In a wok or large, heavy frying pan over medium–high heat, fry the thick coconut milk, stirring constantly, until it begins to separate, 3–5 minutes. If it does not separate, add the optional oil. Add red curry paste and fry, stirring constantly, until fragrant, 1–2 minutes. Tear 2 kaffir lime leaves and basil into pieces.

Add remaining thin coconut milk to the wok, increase heat, and bring to a gentle boil. Add duck and simmer until heated through, about 5 minutes. Add torn lime leaves, green peppercorns, both varieties of eggplants, pineapple and cherry tomatoes. Reduce heat and simmer for 3 minutes. Add water, if necessary. Add all remaining ingredients, reserving a few basil leaves and the remaining kaffir lime leaf for garnish.

Transfer to a serving bowl, garnish with reserved basil, and drizzle with reserved thick coconut milk. Roll the remaining kaffir lime leaf into a tight cylinder and cut into fine shreds; sprinkle over curry.

Tip

Roasted ducks are readily available in Chinese delicatessens and at numerous Asian markets.

Steamed chicken buns

Makes 16

Dough

2½ cups (10 oz/300 g) all-purpose (plain) flour

3 teaspoons baking powder

½ cup (3¾ oz/110 g) superfine (caster) sugar

½ cup (4 fl oz/125 ml) milk

⅓ cup (3 fl oz/90 ml) water

¼ cup (2 fl oz/60 ml) vegetable oil

Filling

6 Chinese dried mushrooms

1 tablespoon vegetable oil

3 teaspoons peeled and grated fresh ginger

8 oz (250 g) ground (minced) chicken

2 tablespoons chopped, drained canned
   bamboo shoots

4 scallions (shallots/spring onions), chopped

1 tablespoon oyster sauce

1 teaspoon soy sauce

1 teaspoon Asian sesame oil

¼ teaspoon salt

2 teaspoons cornstarch (cornflour) mixed
   with 2 tablespoons chicken stock (see page 220)

For dough: Sift flour and baking powder into a bowl and add sugar. Gradually add combined milk, water and oil, mixing to form a soft dough. Turn out onto a floured work surface and knead until smooth, 1–2 minutes. Wrap dough in plastic wrap and chill for 1 hour.

For filling: Place mushrooms in a small bowl, add boiling water to cover and allow to stand until softened, 10–15 minutes. Drain, squeeze excess liquid from mushrooms and finely chop, discarding thick stems. In a wok or frying pan, heat oil over medium heat, and fry ginger until aromatic, about 1 minute. Add ground chicken and cook until meat changes color, about 3 minutes. Stir in bamboo shoots, scallions, oyster sauce, soy sauce, sesame oil, salt and cornstarch mixture. Bring to a boil and stir until sauce thickens. Remove from heat, transfer filling to a plate and allow to cool completely.

Roll dough into a sausage shape 16 inches (40.5 cm) long. Cut into 16 1-inch (2.5-cm) pieces and roll each into a ball. Cover with a damp kitchen towel. Working with one piece of dough at a time, press into a cup shape. Place 1 tablespoon of filling in the center of dough. Gather edges together, twist and seal. Cover with a damp kitchen towel and repeat with remaining dough.

Cut out 16 squares of parchment (baking paper) and place buns, sealed side down, on paper. Half fill a medium wok with water (steamer should not touch water) and bring to a boil. Working in batches, arrange buns in steamer, cover and place steamer over boiling water. Steam for 20 minutes, adding more boiling water to wok when necessary. Lift steamer off wok and carefully remove buns.

Step-by-step basic buns

1. Divide dough into walnut-sized rounds.

2. Roll or press each piece out to a circle. Cover dough with a damp kitchen towel to prevent it from drying out.

3. Working with one dough round at a time, spoon filling into the center. Gather edges together and twist to seal dough. Cut out squares of parchment (baking paper) and place buns, sealed side down, onto paper.

Stir-fried chicken in roasted curry paste sauce

Serves 4–6

2 tablespoons vegetable oil

2 rounded tablespoons red curry paste (see page 231)

4 garlic cloves, chopped

2 shallots, sliced

1 lb (500 g) boned and skinned chicken breasts, cut into 1½-inch (3.5-cm) cubes

1 teaspoon sugar

3 tablespoons fish sauce

½–¾ cup (2 ½–4 fl oz/80–125 ml) thin coconut milk or water

20 basil leaves

steamed rice, for serving

In a wok, heat half the oil, swirling to coat the sides. Stir-fry the curry paste, garlic and shallots over medium heat for 2–3 minutes. Add the chicken and stir-fry briefly, basting to coat each piece.

In a bowl, combine the sugar, fish sauce and coconut milk, and add to the chicken. Bring to a boil, stirring constantly. Add the basil leaves, and toss.

Serve immediately with steamed rice.

Stir-fried ginger chicken

Serves 6

6 whole boneless chicken breasts

2 tablespoons fish sauce

2 tablespoons soy sauce

1 teaspoon sugar

2 tablespoons vegetable oil

1 red onion, sliced

6 garlic cloves, chopped

2-inch (5-cm) piece fresh ginger, peeled and
   thinly sliced

3 red or green serrano chilies, stemmed and
   cut lengthwise into fine strips

¼ teaspoon red chili flakes

¼ cup (½ oz/15 g) coarsely chopped mint
   or basil leaves

whole mint or basil leaves, for garnish

steamed rice, for serving

Cut the chicken breasts into 1½ x 1 x ½-inch
(3.5 x 2.5 x 1-cm) pieces. Set aside.

In a bowl, combine the fish sauce, soy sauce and sugar.
Set aside.

In a wok, warm oil over medium heat, add the onion and
garlic and sauté until golden brown. Add the chicken pieces
and stir-fry until white and opaque. Add the ginger, chilies,
chili flakes and fish sauce mixture and cook until chicken is
just cooked through, about 4 minutes. Transfer to a serving
plate.

Garnish with mint or basil leaves and serve immediately
with rice.

Sweet chicken wings

Serves 4

6 chicken wings, wing tips removed

pinch sesame salt

1 tablespoon ginger juice (obtained by grating
fresh ginger)

¼ cup (1 oz/30 g) cornstarch (cornflour)

1½ cups (12 fl oz/375 ml) vegetable or sunflower oil,
for frying

2 tablespoons light soy sauce

1 tablespoon malt liquid (mullyeot)

1 tablespoon sugar

1 teaspoon ginger juice (obtained by grating
fresh ginger)

1 tablespoon rice wine

3 tablespoons water

5 whole cloves garlic

2 fresh red chilies, halved lengthwise, seeds removed

2 fresh green chilies, halved lengthwise, seeds removed

Asian sesame oil to taste

Wash chicken wings and pat dry with paper towels.
Combine sesame salt and 1 tablespoon ginger juice in a
bowl, then add chicken wings. Mix well to coat in juice.
Remove wings and coat with cornstarch.

In a wok or deep frying pan, heat oil until very hot. Fry
wings until golden, about 10 minutes. Remove from oil and
drain on paper towels.

In a wok, combine soy sauce, malt liquid, sugar,
1 teaspoon ginger juice, rice wine and water and bring to a
boil. Add garlic and red and green chilies and stir in well.
Continue boiling sauce until reduced by half. Add chicken
wings and mix to coat with sauce. Transfer chicken wings,
garlic and chilies to a serving plate, sprinkle with sesame oil
and serve with steamed rice.

Sweet-and-sour chicken and noodles

Serves 4

8 oz (250 g) rice stick noodles

vegetable oil for deep-frying, plus 2 tablespoons

8 oz (250 g) skinless chicken breast fillet, cut into
   1-inch (2.5-cm) pieces

1 onion, sliced

2 tablespoons tomato paste (purée)

2 tablespoons palm sugar or brown sugar

1 tablespoon fish sauce

3 tablespoons lime juice

1 piece grapefruit zest (rind), 2 inches (5 cm) long,
   shredded

2 tablespoons water

2 tablespoons cilantro (fresh coriander) leaves

thin strips grapefruit zest (rind), for garnish

lime wedges, for serving

Place noodles in plastic bag and roughly break up into bite-sized pieces.

In a wok or frying pan, heat oil until it reaches 375°F (190°C) on a deep-frying thermometer or until a small bread cube dropped in oil sizzles and turns golden. Working in batches if necessary, add noodles and fry until golden and crisp, about 30 seconds. Using slotted spoon, remove from pan and drain on paper towels.

In another wok over medium–high heat, warm 2 tablespoons oil. Add chicken and cook, stirring occasionally, until golden, 4–5 minutes. Remove from pan. Add onion to same pan and cook until softened, about 2 minutes.

In a small bowl, combine tomato paste, sugar, fish sauce, lime juice, shredded zest and water. Add to pan, reduce heat to low and simmer, stirring occasionally, until sauce thickens, 3–4 minutes. Stir in chicken and noodles, raise heat to medium and cook until heated through, 1–2 minutes.

To serve, spoon chicken and noodles onto individual plates. Sprinkle with cilantro leaves and garnish with zest strips. Accompany with lime wedges.

Teriyaki chicken

Serves 4

4 boneless chicken breasts

½ cup (2½ oz/75 g) all-purpose (plain) flour

2 tablespoons vegetable oil

½ cup (4 fl oz/125 ml) Teriyaki sauce (see page 225)

2 cups (16 oz/500 g) hot cooked rice

1 teaspoon sesame seeds, toasted

2 scallions (shallots/spring onions), thinly sliced,
   for garnish

nori, cut into fine strips, for garnish

Remove skin and trim any fat from chicken breasts. Place each breast on a cutting board and pound gently with a meat mallet to flatten slightly. Place flour on a plate. Dredge chicken in flour.

In a wok, heat oil over high heat. Add chicken and brown well on both sides, about 4 minutes. Remove breasts from pan and place in a clean wok with teriyaki sauce. Bring sauce to a boil, then reduce heat to low and simmer, covered, turning chicken three times, until cooked through, about 5 minutes. Remove from pan and cut into slices ½ inch (12 mm) wide.

Divide chicken among 4 plates with rice and top with teriyaki sauce from pan. Garnish with toasted sesame seeds, scallions and nori strips.

Thai curry with chicken

Serves 4–6

1 tablespoon sticky (glutinous) rice

¼ cup (2 fl oz/60 ml) vegetable oil

¼ cup (2 fl oz/60 ml) red curry paste (see page 231)

12 oz (375 g) boneless chicken thighs or breasts,
  thinly sliced

½ cup (2 oz/60 g) chopped eggplant (aubergine)
  or 1 round eggplant or ¼ long green eggplant

¼ cup (1 oz/30 g) pea eggplants (optional)

2 long beans or 6–8 green beans, cut into
  1-inch (2.5-cm) pieces

2 cups (16 fl oz/500 ml) chicken stock (see page 220)
  or water

2 tablespoons fish sauce

7 fresh eryngo (sawtooth coriander) leaves
  or 6 sprigs cilantro (fresh coriander), coarsely
  chopped or torn

4 fresh piper (beetle) leaves, or 2 cabbage leaves,
  coarsely chopped

1 cup fresh acacia leaves, coarsely chopped (optional)

1 fresh long red chili, seeded and cut into large pieces

¼ teaspoon salt

In a wok or small frying pan over low heat, stir rice until golden brown, 3–5 minutes. Transfer to a mortar and pulverize with a pestle; set aside.

In a wok or large, heavy frying pan, heat oil over medium–high heat and fry curry paste, stirring constantly, until fragrant, 1–2 minutes. Add chicken and stir-fry until opaque on all sides, about 2 minutes. Add eggplants and beans; stir together well.

Add 1 cup (8 fl oz/250 ml) chicken stock or water; simmer for 2 minutes. Add remaining stock or water, fish sauce, remaining ingredients and ground rice. Bring to a boil, reduce heat, and simmer 2 minutes for chicken breasts, 5–7 minutes for thighs. Transfer to a serving bowl and serve.

Tips

- In Thailand, the availability of local ingredients allows for variations to this dish. For example, this recipe can be made with frog instead of chicken.
- In the north of Thailand, ¼ teaspoon prickly ash (kamchatton) would be added with the chicken stock. Substitute with ¼ teaspoon Szechuan peppercorns if desired.

beef, lamb and pork

Beef braised in rice wine

Serves 4

⅓ cup (3 fl oz/90 ml) dry rice wine or dry sherry
3 tablespoons fish sauce
1 teaspoon sugar
2 teaspoons ground pepper
2 lb (1 kg) boneless beef blade or chuck, trimmed
    and cut into 1-inch (2.5-cm) cubes
    (see Tips below)
3 tablespoons vegetable oil
½ cup (2 oz/60 g) brown or pink shallots (French
    shallots), crushed
cloves from ½ bulb garlic, crushed
2 sticks cinnamon, or ½ teaspoon ground cinnamon
½ teaspoon aniseed
about 1¼ cups (10 fl oz/310 ml) water
3 tomatoes, peeled and seeded
¼ cup (2 oz/60 g) butter
¼ cup (1 oz/30 g) all-purpose (plain) flour
cilantro (fresh coriander) sprigs, for garnish (optional)
crusty bread rolls or baguette, for serving

In a glass or earthenware bowl, combine rice wine, fish sauce, sugar and 1 teaspoon pepper. Stir to blend. Add beef and let stand at room temperature for 2 hours, or cover and refrigerate for up to 24 hours. Stir several times during this period. Using a slotted spoon, transfer beef from marinade and pat dry; reserve marinade.

In a large wok, heat oil over medium heat and sauté half of shallots and half of garlic until soft, about 3 minutes. Using a slotted spoon, transfer to a bowl. Add half of beef and cook, stirring frequently, until all sides are lightly seared, about 5 minutes. Using a slotted spoon, transfer to a bowl. Repeat with remaining meat.

In same wok, combine meat, cinnamon, aniseed and cooked shallots and add remaining garlic. Add 1 cup (8 fl oz/250 ml) water plus any marinade. Cover and simmer over medium-low heat just until beef is tender, about

2 hours. Shake occasionally to prevent scorching. If the braise cooks dry, add a little more water.

Meanwhile, peel and seed tomatoes: Use a small knife to cut away and remove each tomato core. Turn tomato over and lightly score underside with an X. Plunge into a large pot of rapidly boiling water and cook for exactly 10 seconds. Remove immediately from water and plunge into ice water to stop cooking. The skin should now pull easily from pulp; discard. Cut tomatoes in half and squeeze over a strainer to extract all seeds. Discard seeds and retain tomatoes and juice.

In a medium saucepan, combine tomatoes, strained tomato juice and remaining raw shallots, garlic and 1 teaspoon pepper. Add remaining ¼ cup (2 fl oz/60 ml) water and cook until tomatoes are just starting to break up, about 3 minutes. In a separate saucepan, melt butter over low heat and whisk in flour. Cook, stirring constantly, until it barely begins to brown, about 2–3 minutes. Whisk into tomato mixture and remove from heat.

When beef is barely tender, remove cinnamon sticks, if using, from braise. Stir in tomato mixture. Reduce heat to a simmer, cover, and cook until fork tender, 30–60 minutes. If desired, garnish with cilantro sprigs. Serve with bread rolls or baguette.

Tips
- Inexpensive beef cuts work best in this braised dish. Do not use premium cuts like loin (saddle), or lean meat like round (topside), as they can become tough and dry during long, slow cooking.
- This is a classic example of Vietnamese fusion food, created, presumably, after the French colonists' departure, when red wine flowed less freely and the local substitute of rice wine was used. This recipe's European prototype is arguably boeuf bourguignon or a Flemish-style carbonnade.

Beef chow mein

Serves 4–6

6½ oz (200 g) wheat flour, rice stick or thick
    egg noodles

2 tablespoons soy sauce

3 tablespoons hoisin sauce

2 cloves garlic, crushed

2 teaspoons peeled and grated fresh ginger

12 oz (375 g) round (topside) or sirloin (rump) steak,
    thinly sliced

2 tablespoons vegetable oil

8 fresh shiitake mushrooms, brushed clean and sliced

6 scallions (shallots/spring onions), sliced

6 oz (180 g) broccoli, cut into florets

2 tablespoons beef stock (see page 220)

1 tablespoon dry sherry

1 teaspoon Asian sesame oil

Cook noodles, then drain and set aside. In glass or ceramic bowl, combine soy and hoisin sauces, garlic and ginger. Add steak slices, turn to coat in marinade, cover and marinate for 30 minutes. Drain and reserve marinade.

In a wok or frying pan over medium–high heat, warm vegetable oil. Add steak and stir-fry until meat changes color, 3–4 minutes. Remove from wok or pan. Return wok or pan to medium–high heat, add mushrooms, scallions and broccoli, and stir-fry for 2 minutes. Add noodles, steak, reserved marinade, stock, sherry and sesame oil. Cook until heated through, 1–2 minutes.

Serve immediately, divided among individual plates.

Beef kabobs

Serves 4

7 oz (220 g) beef tenderloin or scotch fillet
1 oz/30 g scallions (shallots/spring onions)
1 green bell pepper (capsicum)
4 skewers, 5 inches (12 cm) long, soaked in water
    for 30 minutes
vegetable or sunflower oil, for frying
lettuce leaves, for serving

For marinade
2 tablespoons light soy sauce
2 teaspoons sugar
1 scallion (shallot/spring onion), finely chopped
1 teaspoon pan-toasted, ground sesame seeds
    to a powder
1 teaspoon sesame oil

Cut beef into strips about ¾ inch (2 cm) wide by ¼ inch (6 mm) thick by 2½ inches (6 cm) long. Score surface with the tip of a sharp knife.

To make marinade: In a medium glass or ceramic bowl, combine soy sauce, sugar, chopped scallions, sesame seeds and sesame oil. Mix beef strips in marinade and marinate for 15–20 minutes.

Cut scallions into strips 2 inches (5 cm) long. Remove core and seeds from bell pepper and cut into slices 2 inches (5 cm) long.

Thread alternate pieces of beef, scallions and bell pepper alternately onto each skewer, leaving about 1¼ inches (3 cm) free for holding skewer.

In a wok over a high heat, heat 1 tablespoon oil. Fry kabobs for 2 minutes on each side. Arrange lettuce leaves on a serving plate, place kabobs in center and serve.

Beef stir-fry on crisp noodles

Serves 4

vegetable oil for deep-frying, plus 1 tablespoon

8 oz (250 g) fresh thin egg noodles

1 tablespoon soy sauce

3 cloves garlic, chopped

12 oz (375 g) sirloin (rump) steak, thinly sliced

2 onions, cut into eighths

6–7 oz (180–220 g) asparagus, trimmed and cut
    into 1-inch (2.5-cm) pieces

2 tablespoons oyster sauce

1 teaspoon cornstarch (cornflour) mixed with
    2 tablespoons beef stock (see page 220)

In a wok or frying pan, heat oil until it reaches 375°F
(190°C) on a deep-frying thermometer or until a small bread
cube dropped in oil sizzles and turns golden. Working in
batches, add noodles and fry until crisp, about 30 seconds.
Using a slotted spoon, remove from pan and drain on
paper towels.

In a glass or ceramic bowl, combine soy sauce and garlic.
Add steak slices, turn to coat with marinade, cover and
marinate for 30 minutes. Drain and reserve marinade.

In a wok or frying pan over medium–high heat, warm
1 tablespoon oil. Add steak and stir-fry until meat changes
color, 3–4 minutes, remove from pan. Return pan to
medium–high heat, add onion and stir-fry until softened,
about 2 minutes. Return meat to pan, add asparagus and
cook until asparagus is tender-crisp, about 2 minutes. Stir
in oyster sauce and cornstarch and stock. Continuing to
stir, cook until sauce thickens, 1–2 minutes.

To serve, arrange noodles on individual plates. Top with
beef stir-fry and serve immediately.

Beef stir-fry with Chinese greens

Serves 4

10½ oz (315 g) sirloin (rump) or round (topside) steak

3 tablespoons vegetable oil

4 cloves garlic, crushed

1 tablespoon peeled and grated fresh ginger

2 small red chilies, seeded and chopped

1 bunch Chinese broccoli or 6 celery stalks, trimmed
   and cut into 1¼-inch (3-cm) lengths

7 oz (220 g) sugar snap peas or snow peas
   (mange-tout), trimmed

3½ oz (105 g) fresh bean sprouts, rinsed

1 tablespoon oyster sauce

1 teaspoon sambal oelek (see page 230)

steamed white rice, for serving

Enclose steak in freezer wrap and freeze until slightly firm, about 30 minutes. Remove from freezer and thinly slice. In a bowl, combine beef, 1 tablespoon vegetable oil, garlic and ginger. Cover and refrigerate for 30 minutes.

Drain beef from marinade, discarding marinade. In a wok over medium–high heat, warm remaining 2 tablespoons vegetable oil. Working in batches, add beef and stir-fry until brown, 1–2 minutes. Remove from wok and drain on paper towels. Add chilies, broccoli or celery, sugar snap peas or snow peas and bean sprouts and stir-fry until tender-crisp, 2–3 minutes. Add beef, oyster sauce and sambal oelek. Stir-fry until heated through, about 1 minute.

Serve hot, accompanied with steamed white rice.

Beef with bamboo shoots

Serves 4

2 tablespoons vegetable oil

2½ lbs (1.25 kg) sirloin or round steak, thinly sliced

2 small fresh red chilies, chopped

2 cloves garlic, minced

1 tablespoon very finely chopped fresh lemongrass

1 teaspoon grated fresh ginger

2 tablespoons Thai fish sauce

1 tablespoon soy sauce

1 can (12 oz/375 g) bamboo shoots, drained

2 tablespoons chopped fresh basil

2 scallions (spring onions/shallots), chopped

cooked rice or noodles, for serving

In a large wok, heat oil over high heat. Add meat in batches (to ensure even browning and so that the meat does not cook in its own juices) and stir-fry until browned all over. Add chilies, garlic, lemongrass and ginger and stir-fry until fragrant, about 2 minutes. Stir in sauces and bamboo shoots and stir-fry until bamboo shoots are just starting to soften, about 2 minutes. Stir in basil and scallions. Serve immediately on a bed of rice or noodles.

Beef with basil leaves

Serves 4–6

3 tablespoons vegetable oil

15 cloves garlic, crushed

10 fresh red or green chilies, coarsely chopped

1 lb (500 g) ground (minced) beef

1 tablespoon oyster sauce

2 tablespoons fish sauce

1 teaspoon sweet (thick) soy sauce

1 tablespoon granulated (white) sugar (or to taste)

2 fresh long red chilies, cut into large pieces

1 cup (8 fl oz/250 ml) chicken stock (see page 220)
   or water

1½ cups (1½ oz/45 g) loosely packed fresh basil
   leaves, preferably holy basil

In a wok or large, heavy frying pan, heat oil over high heat. Add garlic and chilies and stir-fry until garlic just begins to brown.

Add beef, stirring vigorously to break it up, about 2 minutes. Add oyster sauce, fish sauce, sweet soy sauce, and sugar to taste. Stir well to combine, then add chilies.

Add chicken stock or water and bring to a boil. Add basil, cook for 1 minute, then remove from heat.

Transfer to a serving plate and serve.

Tip

For a less piquant dish, keep the chilies whole, or seed them.

Chinese barbecue pork stir-fry

Serves 4

3 oz (90 g) cellophane (bean thread) noodles

1 tablespoon vegetable oil

6 scallions (shallots/spring onions), cut into
   1-inch (2.5-cm) pieces

1 red bell pepper (capsicum), seeded and sliced

4 oz (125 g) Chinese barbecue pork, sliced

2 bok choy or Chinese broccoli, trimmed

1½ cups (6 oz/180 g) fresh beans sprouts, rinsed

2 tablespoons soy sauce

Soak noodles in boiling water for 10 minutes. Drain and set aside. In a wok or frying pan, heat oil over medium–high heat. Add scallions and bell pepper and cook until softened, about 2 minutes. Add pork and bok choy and stir-fry until pork is tender, about 2 minutes. Stir in noodles, bean sprouts and soy sauce. Cook until heated through, about 1 minute.

Serve hot, divided among individual plates.

Chinese beef and vegetable stir-fry

Serves 4

1 oz (30 g) dried shiitake mushrooms, soaked
   in boiling water for 20 minutes
2 tablespoons sunflower oil
4 oz (115 g) snow peas (mange-tout)
4 oz (115 g) whole baby corn cobs
4 oz (115 g) bean sprouts
1 large bunch scallions (shallots), chopped
1 red bell pepper (capsicum), seeded and sliced
1¼ lb (550 g) rib-eye steak, thinly sliced
2 tablespoons oyster sauce
2 tablespoons Chinese rice wine or dry sherry
3 tablespoons light soy sauce
3 tablespoons beef stock (see page 220)
1 tablespoon cornstarch (cornflour)
fried rice or noodles, for serving

Drain and dry mushrooms and cut in half if large.

In a large wok or frying pan, heat 1 tablespoon oil. Stir-fry mushrooms, snow peas, corn, bean sprouts, scallions and bell pepper for 2–3 minutes, then remove from pan.

Heat remaining oil. Stir-fry beef until brown, 2–3 minutes. Return vegetables to pan. In a bowl, combine oyster sauce, rice wine, soy sauce, stock and cornstarch. Pour into pan, mix well, and bring to a boil, stirring continuously.

Transfer to a warmed serving dish and serve immediately with fried rice or noodles.

Dry beef curry with sweet potato

Serves 4

1 onion, chopped

2 cloves garlic

1 teaspoon shrimp paste

1 teaspoon ground cumin

2 teaspoons ground coriander

1 tablespoon chopped lemongrass

½ teaspoon ground turmeric

1 teaspoon ground paprika

1 teaspoon grated lime zest (rind)

2 tablespoons vegetable oil

11 oz (330 g) sirloin (rump) or round (topside) steak,
   cut into 1¼-inch (3-cm) cubes

1 cup (8 fl oz/250 ml) water

7 oz (220 g) sweet potato, peeled and finely diced

1 long red chili, seeded and sliced

1 long green chili, seeded and sliced

steamed white rice, for serving

In a food processor, combine onion, garlic, shrimp paste, cumin, coriander, lemongrass, turmeric, paprika and lime zest. Process until smooth. Set aside.

In a wok over medium–high heat, warm vegetable oil. Working in batches, add beef and stir-fry until brown, 3–4 minutes. Remove from wok and drain on paper towels. Add spice blend to wok and cook until aromatic, about 1 minute.

Add beef and water and bring to a boil. Reduce heat to low, cover and simmer, stirring occasionally, for 30 minutes. Stir in sweet potato and simmer, uncovered, until sweet potato is tender, about 10 minutes. (Add a little more water if necessary.)

To serve, divide among individual plates and sprinkle with sliced chilies. Accompany with steamed white rice.

Fried pork in endive

Serves 4

1 tablespoon vegetable oil

2 cloves garlic, crushed

1 tablespoon peeled and grated fresh ginger

6 scallions (shallots/spring onions), chopped

½ teaspoon shrimp paste

1 tablespoon chopped lemongrass

2 teaspoons sambal oelek (see page 230)

7 oz (220 g) pork fillet, finely chopped

8 oz (250 g) cherry tomatoes, quartered

1 tablespoon coconut milk

3 tablespoons chopped cilantro (fresh coriander)

3 heads Belgian endive (chicory/witloof), cored and
   leaves separated

In a wok over medium heat, warm vegetable oil. Add garlic, ginger, scallions, shrimp paste, lemongrass and sambal oelek and stir-fry until aromatic, about 2 minutes. Add pork and cook until pork changes color, about 3 minutes.

Stir in tomatoes and coconut milk and stir-fry until tomatoes soften slightly, 1–2 minutes. Remove from heat and stir in cilantro.

To serve, spoon pork filling into endive leaves. Divide among individual plates and serve hot.

Ginger pork

Serves 4

½ cup (4 oz/124 g) sugar

½ cup (4 fl oz/125 ml) soy sauce

1 teaspoon mirin

2 tablespoons chicken stock (see page 220) or water

1 lb (500 g) pork fillet, trimmed of sinew, cut into
  slices ½ inch (12 mm) thick

½ cup (2½ oz/ 75 g) peeled and finely grated fresh
  ginger

2 tablespoons vegetable oil

2 scallions (shallots/spring onions), thinly sliced

1 teaspoon sesame seeds, for garnish

In a small saucepan over medium–high heat, combine sugar, soy sauce, mirin and stock or water and bring to a boil, stirring to dissolve sugar. Remove sauce from heat and set aside.

Dip both sides of each pork slice into grated ginger. Reserve any leftover ginger. In a wok, heat oil over medium–high heat. Add pork and fry, turning once until pork is no longer pink, 3–4 minutes. Add sauce to pan with any remaining grated ginger and bring to a boil. Reduce heat to low and simmer for 1 minute. Remove pork from pan and divide among 4 warmed plates. Spoon any remaining sauce from pan over slices. Garnish with sliced scallions and sprinkle with sesame seeds. Serve immediately.

Lamb with dried fruit

Serves 5–6

2 lb (1 kg) boneless lamb shoulder

¼ cup (2 oz/60 g) ghee or ¼ cup (2 fl oz/60 ml)
   vegetable oil

1 medium yellow (brown) onion, chopped

2 cups (16 fl oz/500 ml) water

salt

small piece cinnamon stick

1 dried lime or zest (rind) from ½ lemon

½ cup (3 oz/90 g) chopped pitted dates

¾ cup (4 oz/125 g) dried apricots

¾ cup (4 oz/125 g) dried prunes, pitted

¼ cup (1½ oz/45 g) golden raisins (sultanas)

2 tablespoons brown sugar

steamed rice, for serving

Cut lamb into ¾-inch (2-cm) cubes. In a heavy saucepan over high heat, heat half of the ghee or oil. Add lamb and cook, turning as needed, until browned on all sides, 8–10 minutes.

Push meat to one side, add onion and cook for 5 minutes. Reduce heat to low and add 1 cup (8 fl oz/250 ml) water, salt to taste, cinnamon stick and dried lime (pierced twice with a skewer) or lemon zest. Cover and simmer 45 minutes.

Place chopped dates in a small pan with remaining 1 cup (8 fl oz/250 ml) water. Set over low heat until dates soften. Press through a sieve into a bowl to purée.

Add date purée, apricots, prunes, raisins and brown sugar to pan. Stir to combine, cover tightly and simmer until lamb is tender, about 1 hour. Add more water during this time if the meat and fruit seem dry.

Remove cinnamon and dried lime or lemon zest and discard. Serve lamb with steamed rice.

Tip

When dates are being dried, they exude a thick syrup resembling molasses. Iraqi cooks add some of the syrup to this dish. Soaked and puréed, dried dates with brown sugar added, provide a similar flavor.

Long beans with pork and red curry paste

Serves 4

¼ cup (2 fl oz/60 ml) vegetable oil

1 cup (8 fl oz/250 ml) commercial or fresh red curry
   paste (see page 231)

20 oz (625 g) boneless pork butt or loin, thinly sliced

15 kaffir lime leaves, stemmed

1 lb (500 g) long beans or green beans, cut into 1-inch
   (2.5-cm) pieces

5 fresh long red chilies, seeded and cut into strips

1 tablespoon palm sugar

2 tablespoons granulated (white) sugar

¼ cup (2 fl oz/60 ml) fish sauce

1 cup (1 oz/30 g) loosely packed fresh sweet Thai basil
   leaves, coarsely torn

In a wok or large, heavy skillet, heat oil over medium–high heat. Add curry paste and cook, stirring constantly, until fragrant, 1–2 minutes. Add meat and stir until opaque on all sides, 2–3 minutes. Add 10 kaffir lime leaves, beans, and chilies. Cook, stirring frequently, for about 2 minutes, or until meat is barely tender.

Add palm sugar—if using a wok, add it along the edge of the wok so that it melts before stirring into the other ingredients; if using a standard saucepan, add directly to the pan. Add granulated sugar, then fish sauce and basil. Stir well, then remove from heat and transfer to a platter.

Roll remaining kaffir lime leaves into a tight cylinder and cut into fine shreds. Sprinkle over the dish and serve.

Meatballs in tomato sauce

Serves 5–6

1½ lb (750 g) finely ground (minced) beef or lamb

1 clove garlic, crushed

1 small yellow (brown) onion, finely grated

2 thick slices stale white Italian bread, crusts removed

1 egg

1 teaspoon ground cumin

2 tablespoons finely chopped fresh flat-leaf (Italian) parsley

salt

freshly ground black pepper

all-purpose (plain) flour, for coating

¼ cup (2 oz/60 g) butter or ¼ cup (2 fl oz/60 ml) olive oil

1½ cups (9 oz/280 g) chopped, peeled tomatoes

½ cup (2½ oz/75 g) finely chopped green bell pepper (capsicum)

½ teaspoon sugar

½ cup (4 fl oz/125 ml) water

steamed rice, for serving

In a bowl, combine beef or lamb with garlic and onion. Soak bread in cold water, squeeze dry and crumble into bowl. Add egg, cumin, parsley and salt and pepper to taste. Mix thoroughly to a smooth paste. With moistened hands, form 1 tablespoon portions of meat mixture into oval, sausagelike shapes. Coat lightly with flour.

In a deep wok or frying pan over high heat, heat butter or oil and fry meatballs until lightly browned on all sides. Remove to a plate. Add tomatoes and bell pepper to wok or frying pan and cook over medium heat for 5 minutes. Add sugar and season with salt and pepper to taste, then stir in water. Bring sauce to a boil and return meatballs to wok or pan. Reduce heat to low. Cover and simmer until meatballs are tender and sauce is thick, about 1 hour.

Serve immediately with steamed rice.

Pork and lime patties

Serves 4

8 oz (250 g) ground (minced) pork

2 teaspoons fish sauce

1 teaspoon oyster sauce

2 teaspoons sambal oelek (see page 230)

1 egg white, lightly beaten

2 cloves garlic, crushed

2 tablespoons cornstarch (cornflour)

2 teaspoon grated lime zest (rind)

4 kaffir lime leaves, shredded

¼ cup (1 oz/30 g) chopped scallions
   (shallots/spring onions)

½ cup (4 fl oz/125 ml) vegetable oil, for frying

sweet chili sauce, for serving

In a bowl, combine pork, fish sauce, oyster sauce, sambal oelek and egg white. Mix well. Add garlic, cornstarch, lime zest, lime leaves and scallions. Using moistened hands, mix until well combined. Divide mixture into 16 pieces and shape into patties.

In a wok over medium heat, warm vegetable oil. Working in batches, add pork patties and fry, turning once, until tender and golden on both sides, 6–8 minutes. Drain on paper towels.

Serve hot with sweet chili sauce.

Pork and nectarine stir-fry

Serves 4–6

2 tablespoons vegetable oil

3 cloves garlic, crushed

1 small red chili, seeded and chopped

1 lb (500 g) pork fillet, thinly sliced

1 bunch choy sum or spinach, trimmed and cut into
   1¼-inch (3-cm) lengths

3 kaffir lime leaves, shredded

2½ tablespoons light soy sauce

2 teaspoons lime juice

2 firm nectarines, pitted and sliced

steamed white rice, for serving

In a wok over medium–high heat, warm vegetable oil. Add garlic and chili and stir-fry until aromatic, about 1 minute. Add pork, choy sum or spinach and lime leaves and stir-fry until pork changes color, 3–4 minutes. Add soy sauce, lime juice and nectarines and stir-fry until heated through, 1–2 minutes.

Serve hot, accompanied with steamed white rice.

Pumpkin with pork

Serves 4–6

⅓ cup (3 fl oz/90 ml) vegetable oil

9 cloves garlic, crushed

1 lb (500 g) pumpkin or squash, peeled, seeded,
    and thinly sliced

½ cup (4 fl oz/125 ml) chicken stock (see page 220)
    or water

12 oz (375 g) boneless pork loin, cut into thin strips

¼ cup (2 fl oz/60 ml) fish sauce

2 eggs, lightly beaten

fresh sweet Thai basil leaves, for garnish

In a wok or large, heavy frying pan, heat oil over
medium–high heat. Add garlic, pumpkin or squash, and
chicken stock or water. Bring to a boil.

Add pork, reduce heat, and simmer until meat is opaque
throughout and pumpkin or squash is tender, about
5 minutes. Add fish sauce, then stir in eggs to just bind
sauce.

Transfer to a serving dish, garnish with basil leaves and
serve.

Tip

For a spectacular presentation, serve this dish in a
hollowed-out pumpkin.

Red curry beef

Serves 4

8 oz (250 g) sirloin (rump) or round (topside) steak
1 tablespoon vegetable oil
1 tablespoon red curry paste (see page 231)
1 cup (8 fl oz/250 ml) coconut milk
2 teaspoons fish sauce
1 teaspoon palm sugar or brown sugar
1 cup (6 oz/180 g) drained canned baby corn
⅓ cup (2 oz/60 g) drained canned straw mushrooms
½ cup (½ oz/15 g) small fresh basil leaves
steamed white rice, for serving

Enclose steak in freezer wrap and freeze until slightly firm, about 30 minutes. Remove from freezer and thinly slice. In a wok, heat oil over medium–high heat. Working in batches, add beef and stir-fry until brown, 1–2 minutes. Remove from wok and drain on paper towels. Add curry paste to wok and cook until paste bubbles, 10–15 seconds. Stir in coconut milk, fish sauce, sugar, corn and mushrooms. Bring to a boil, reduce heat and simmer, uncovered, for 5 minutes. Add beef and stir-fry until heated through, about 1 minute.

Spoon into bowls and sprinkle each serving with basil leaves. Serve hot, accompanied with steamed white rice.

Salt bulgogi

Serves 4

½ cup (4 fl oz/125 ml) pear juice
   or ½ cup (4 oz/125 g) grated pear (preferably nashi)
3 tablespoons rice wine
2 lb (1 kg) beef tenderloin (fillet) or scotch fillet
2 tablespoons table salt
3 tablespoons sugar
3 tablespoons finely chopped scallions
   (shallots/spring onions)
2 tablespoons crushed garlic
1 tablespoon pan-toasted, ground sesame seeds
freshly ground black pepper to taste
3 tablespoons sesame oil
1 scallion (shallot/spring onion)
1 fresh red chili
1 tablespoon sesame oil
shiso leaves or lettuce leaves, for serving

Combine pear juice and rice wine in a medium glass or ceramic bowl. Slice beef into strips ¼ inch (6 mm) thick. Add to bowl and let stand for 30 minutes.

Combine salt, sugar, scallions, garlic, sesame seeds, pepper and 3 tablespoons sesame oil in a large glass or ceramic bowl.

Drain beef, add to marinade and mix well. Cover and refrigerate to marinate for 2–3 hours.

Cut scallion into 1½-inch (4-cm) sections, then slice lengthwise into very thin strips. Place in a bowl of cold water for a few seconds, then drain. Slice chili in half lengthwise, remove seeds and membrane and slice into thin strips. In a wok, heat 1 tablespoon sesame oil over medium heat. Remove beef strips from marinade and stir-fry to the desired tenderness.

Arrange shiso leaves or lettuce on a plate. Place beef on leaves, sprinkle with scallion and chili strips, and serve with steamed rice.

Tip
As salt bulgogi does not have any sauce, drizzle with a little sesame oil to give it a sheen.

Shredded pork and beansprouts

Serves 4

½ lb (250 g) lean pork
1 tablespoon cornstarch (cornflour)
1 tablespoon light soy sauce
⅓ teaspoon white pepper
3 thin slices fresh ginger
2 scallions (spring onions)
6 oz (180 g) fresh beansprouts
3 tablespoons vegetable oil
1 teaspoon sesame oil
½ cup (3 fl oz/90 ml) chicken stock (see page 220)
1½ teaspoons extra cornstarch (cornflour)

Slice the pork, stack slices together and cut into narrow shreds, place in a dish with cornstarch, soy and pepper, mix well and marinate for 30 minutes.

Cut ginger into fine shreds. Trim scallions, cut into 1½-inch (4-cm) pieces and shred lengthwise. Break roots and seed pods from beansprouts and rinse. Drain well.

In a wok, heat the oils together until very hot. Add pork and stir-fry quickly until it changes appearance. Add the ginger, scallions and beansprouts and stir-fry for 2 minutes on high heat. Add chicken stock and cornstarch, stir on high heat until sauce coats the ingredients.

Sliced beef, mushrooms and vegetables in oyster sauce

Serves 4

1 lb (500 g) rump steak

1½ tablespoons cornstarch (cornflour)

2 tablespoons fish sauce

3 teaspoons sugar

¾ lb (375 g) Chinese green vegetables

3 tablespoons vegetable oil

4 scallions (spring onions), cut into 1-inch (2.5-cm)
  lengths

4 oz (125 g) can baby champignons, drained

¾ cup (6 fl oz/185 ml) beef stock (see page 220)

cracked black pepper to taste

2 tablespoons oyster sauce

Enclose steak in freezer wrap and freeze until slightly firm, about 30 minutes. Remove from freezer and thinly slice. Place in a dish and sprinkle on 1 tablespoon cornstarch, the fish sauce and sugar. Mix well and marinate for 10 minutes.

Cut the vegetables into 3-inch (8-cm) pieces and blanch in boiling water for 3 minutes. Drain.

In a wok, heat the oil and stir-fry the beef until it changes appearance. Add the onion and champignons and the beef stock mixed with remaining cornstarch. Stir over high heat until the sauce thickens. Add the vegetables and heat through in the sauce. Stir in pepper, transfer to a serving dish and evenly pour over the oyster sauce.

Steamed pork ribs

Makes 8 small servings

1 lb (500 g) pork spareribs, trimmed and cut
    into 3¼-inch (8-cm) lengths (ask your butcher
    to prepare these for you)

1 tablespoon rice wine

1 teaspoon salt

2 teaspoons superfine (caster) sugar

1 teaspoon Asian sesame oil

4 cloves garlic, finely chopped

2 tablespoons fermented black beans, washed
    and chopped

½ teaspoon dry chili flakes

2 teaspoons cornstarch (cornflour)

½ red bell pepper (capsicum), seeded and
    finely shredded

Place ribs in a shallow dish. Combine rice wine, salt, sugar, sesame oil, garlic, black beans, chili flakes and cornstarch and mix well. Pour over ribs, cover and refrigerate for 2 hours.

Half fill a medium wok with water (steamer should not touch water) and bring to a boil. Working in batches, place ribs on a heatproof plate and put it into a bamboo steamer. Cover and place steamer over boiling water. Steam until ribs are tender, about 25 minutes, adding more boiling water to wok when necessary. Lift steamer off wok and carefully remove ribs. Garnish with shredded red bell pepper.

Stir-fried beef with eggs

Serves 4

8 oz (250 g) egg noodles
4 tablespoons vegetable oil
3 cloves garlic, crushed
¼ cup (1 oz/30 g) chopped scallions
  (shallots/spring onions)
8 oz (250 g) lean ground (minced) beef
3 tablespoons water
1 tablespoon soy sauce
1 tablespoon oyster sauce
1 teaspoon cornstarch (cornflour) mixed with
  1 tablespoon water
4 butter lettuce leaves, trimmed
4 eggs, soft-boiled, peeled and halved
¼ cup (⅓ oz/10 g) fresh mint leaves, for garnish

Cook noodles as directed on package or on page 29. Drain and pat dry with paper towels.

In a wok or frying pan over medium–high heat, warm 3 tablespoons of oil. Add garlic and cook until aromatic, about 1 minute. Add noodles and stir-fry for 2 minutes. Remove from wok or pan. Add remaining 1 tablespoon oil to wok or pan over medium–high heat. Add scallions and ground beef and stir-fry until meat changes color, 3–4 minutes. Add water, soy and oyster sauces and noodles and stir-fry for 3 minutes. Stir in cornstarch and water and cook, stirring, until sauce thickens, about 2 minutes.

To serve, arrange lettuce leaves on individual plates. Spoon beef and noodles on top. Garnish with egg halves and mint leaves. Serve immediately.

Stir-fried beef with red curry paste

Serves 4

1¼ cups (10 fl oz/300 ml) vegetable oil

¼ cup (2 fl oz/60 ml) commercial or fresh red
  curry paste (see page 231)

1 cup (8 fl oz/250 ml) coconut cream, plus
  2 tablespoons, for serving

12 oz (375 g) beef round, blade, or sirloin, trimmed
  and cut into very thin strips

1 cup (3½ oz/100 g) chopped eggplant (aubergine)
  or 3 round Thai eggplants, quartered then sliced

1 cup (4 oz/125 g) pea eggplants (optional)

¼ cup fresh green peppercorns on stems,
  or 2 tablespoons canned peppercorns, drained

6 kaffir lime leaves, stemmed

2 tablespoons fish sauce

1 tablespoon soy sauce

1 teaspoon granulated (white) sugar

¼ cup (2 fl oz/60 ml) chicken stock (see page 220)
  or water

1 fresh long red chili, coarsely chopped

1 cup (1 oz/30 g) loosely packed fresh sweet
  Thai basil leaves

Heat ¼ cup (2 fl oz/60 ml) oil in a wok or large, heavy
frying pan over medium–high heat. Add curry paste and fry,
stirring constantly, until fragrant, 1–2 minutes. Add ½ cup
(4 fl oz/125 ml) coconut cream, and beef. Stir until gently
boiling. Cook 2 minutes for sirloin, or up to 30 minutes for
tougher cuts like blade.

Add eggplants and peppercorns. Add kaffir lime leaves and
cook, stirring, for 1 minute. Add fish sauce, soy sauce,
sugar, and stock or water. Boil for 1 minute. Stir in the
remaining ½ cup (4 fl oz/125 ml) coconut cream and chili.
Remove from heat. Wash and pat the basil leaves
completely dry with paper towels.

Heat remaining 1 cup (8 fl oz/250 ml) oil in a wok until
surface shimmers. Add basil leaves all at once and fry for a
few seconds, or until lightly crisp. To serve, transfer beef
mixture to a platter, and top with fried basil. Drizzle with
reserved 2 tablespoons coconut cream.

fish and seafood

Braised octopus and onions

Serves 6

1 octopus, about 2 lb (1 kg)
¼ cup (2 fl oz/60 ml) corn oil
1 medium yellow (brown) onion, chopped
2 cloves garlic, finely chopped
1 cup (8 fl oz/250 ml) tomato purée
¼ cup (2 fl oz/60 ml) dry red wine
¼ cup (2 fl oz/60 ml) red wine vinegar
salt
freshly ground black pepper
2 whole cloves
1 cinnamon stick, about 3 inches (8 cm) long
1½ lb (750 g) small boiling (pickling) onions

Pull tentacles from octopus and set aside. Remove intestines, ink sac, eyes and beak and discard. Wash head and tentacles and pull skin from head. Place head and tentacles in a saucepan, cover and cook over medium heat until octopus releases its juice, about 10 minutes. Drain, let cool, and cut into bite-sized pieces.

In a heavy wok, heat oil over medium heat and gently fry chopped onion until translucent, about 7 minutes. Add garlic and octopus and fry for 5 minutes. Add tomato purée, wine, vinegar, salt and pepper to taste, cloves and cinnamon stick. Cover and simmer over low heat for 30 minutes.

Peel boiling (pickling) onions and cut an X in the root end of each. Add to pan; cover and cook until octopus is tender, about 1 hour.

Remove cloves and cinnamon stick, adjust seasonings and serve octopus with steamed rice.

Braised shrimp in ginger-coconut sauce

Serves 4

2 tablespoons peeled and grated fresh ginger

4 cloves garlic, crushed

1 tablespoon ground turmeric

1 small red chili, seeded and chopped

2 tablespoons white vinegar

2 tablespoons peanut oil

2 onions, chopped

1 lb (500 g) jumbo shrimp (king prawns), peeled
   and deveined, tails intact

2 tomatoes, chopped

¾ cup (6 fl oz/180 ml) coconut milk

2 teaspoons cracked black pepper

2 tablespoons chopped fresh cilantro (coriander)

¼ cup (¼ oz/7 g) small whole cilantro (coriander)
   leaves, for garnish

In a food processor or blender, combine ginger, garlic, turmeric, chili and vinegar. Process to form paste.

In a wok over medium-high heat, warm peanut oil. Add onions and spice paste and stir-fry until onions soften, 2 to 3 minutes. Add shrimp and stir-fry until shrimp change color, 3 to 4 minutes. Stir in tomatoes and cook until soft, about 2 minutes. Add coconut milk, reduce heat to low, cover and simmer until sauce thickens slightly and shrimp are tender, 6 to 8 minutes. Stir in pepper and chopped cilantro.

Serve hot, garnished with cilantro leaves.

Cha ca fish with turmeric

Serves 4

3 tablespoons ground turmeric, or a 3-inch (7.5-cm) knob fresh turmeric, peeled and chopped

1-inch (2.5-cm) knob fresh galangal or ginger, peeled

1–2 fresh long red chilies, seeded

2 tablespoons fish sauce

¼ cup (2 fl oz/60 ml) water

1 tablespoon rice vinegar or distilled white vinegar

1 tablespoon sugar, or more to taste

1 lb (500 g) skinless catfish fillets (see Tips), cut into bite-sized pieces

5-oz (150-g) packet dried rice vermicelli (bun), softened and cut into manageable lengths for serving

¼ cup (2 fl oz/60 ml) vegetable oil

1 bunch dill, stemmed and cut into 1½-inch (4-cm) lengths

4 scallions (shallots/spring onions), including green parts, coarsely chopped

½ cup (2 oz/60 g) thinly sliced brown or pink shallots (French shallots)

2 cloves garlic, thinly sliced

⅓ cup (2 oz/60 g) chopped peanuts, lightly toasted

In a mortar, using a pestle, pound turmeric, galangal and chili to a paste. Alternatively, process in a blender or food processor. Add fish sauce, water, vinegar and sugar and stir until dissolved. Pour into a bowl. Add fish, toss to coat, and refrigerate for 3 hours.

Transfer fish to a plate, scrape off marinade and reserve, and pat fish dry with paper towels. In a wok, heat oil over medium–high heat until surface shimmers. Add fish, a few pieces at a time, to hot oil, stirring carefully so as not to break up pieces. Cook until flaky to the touch but not crisp, 1–3 minutes. Using a skimmer, transfer to a platter. Repeat with remaining fish. Reduce heat to medium, add dill and scallions to pan, and stir-fry just until wilted. Place these on top of cooked fish. Quickly stir-fry shallots and garlic in same pan, with any reserved marinade, and spoon on top. Finally, top with crushed peanuts.

Tips

- Ca bong lau and ca lang, varieties of catfish, are used for this dish in Vietnam. Trout substitutes well, as do pike and salmon. Asian alternatives include deep-sea mullet and Taiwanese milk fish.
- To give fish a distinct smoky flavor, it may be grilled then fried, but the grilling is optional. If grilling, cook until opaque throughout, 3–4 minutes, then follow instructions above.

Crab in black bean sauce

Serves 4–6

1 tablespoon peanut oil

3 tablespoons chopped scallions (spring onions/shallots)

2 cloves garlic, chopped

1 teaspoon chopped fresh ginger

1/3 cup (3 fl oz/90 ml) black bean sauce

1/2 cup (4 fl oz/125 ml) fish stock (see page 221)

1 tablespoon sherry (optional)

3 lb (1.5 kg) uncooked crab, segmented and claws cracked

steamed rice, for serving

In a wok or frying pan, heat oil over medium heat. Add scallions, garlic, and ginger and sauté until fragrant, about 1 minute. Pour in sauce, stock, and sherry and bring to a boil. Simmer until slightly thickened, about 4 minutes. Add crab and stir well. Cover and cook 10–15 minutes or until crab is cooked through—to test, crack a shell and see if flesh is tender.

Serve immediately with steamed rice.

Tip

When serving crabs in the shell, it's important to have the claws cracked to allow your guests easy eating. Claws are easily cracked using a nutcracker or meat mallet. Be sure to have lots of finger bowls and hand towels available.

Crab with yellow curry powder

Serves 4–6

1½ lb (750 g) cooked or raw crab in the shell

1 cup (8 fl oz/250 ml) evaporated milk

1 egg, beaten

2 tablespoons soy sauce

½ teaspoon granulated (white) sugar

½ cup (4 fl oz/125 ml) strained chili oil (see page 223)
   or ¼ cup chili oil with ¼ cup vegetable oil

1 teaspoon curry powder

¼ cup (2 fl oz/60 ml) vegetable oil

1 fresh long red chili, cut into strips

4 scallions (shallots/spring onions), coarsely chopped

¼ cup (1 oz/30 g) coarsely chopped Chinese
   or regular celery

Clean crab by pulling off the apron flap on the bottom of the shell. Pry off top shell, remove gills, intestines, and mouth parts. Cut small crabs in half, or large crabs into eight pieces. Twist off claws. Refrigerate until ready to use.

In a medium bowl, combine milk, egg, soy sauce, sugar, chili oil, and curry powder; whisk to blend well.

In a wok or large, heavy frying pan over high heat, heat vegetable oil. Add milk mixture and bring to a boil, stirring constantly. Add crab and cook for 2 minutes, then turn off heat and add chili, scallions, and celery. Spoon into a deep serving dish and serve.

Tip

For a less piquant dish, substitute half the chili oil with vegetable oil and use a mild curry powder.

Crispy fried fish

Serves 4

½ onion, grated

3 cloves garlic, finely chopped

2 teaspoons ground coriander

½ teaspoon chili powder

1 teaspoon ground black pepper

1 tablespoon fresh lemon juice

1 teaspoon sea salt

1 tablespoon vegetable oil

4 white fish fillets (6 oz/185 g each)

1 cup all-purpose (plain) flour

3 cups (24 fl oz/750 ml) vegetable oil, for deep-frying

In a food processor, combine onion, garlic, coriander, chili powder, black pepper, lemon juice, salt, and oil. Process to a paste. Place fish fillets in a baking dish and spread onion paste over fish. Cover and refrigerate for 1 hour.

Place flour in a shallow bowl. Coat fish in flour, shaking off excess. In a large wok, heat oil to 375°F (190°C), or until a small bread cube dropped in the oil sizzles and turns golden in 1 minute. Fry the fish in batches until golden, 1–2 minutes. Using a slotted spoon, transfer to paper towels to drain. Serve immediately, with lime and tomato wedges.

Fish curry

Serves 6

1½ lb (750 g) fish steaks or fillets
salt
2 tablespoons ghee or oil
2 medium-sized yellow (brown) onions, chopped
1 teaspoon peeled and grated fresh ginger
2 cloves garlic, crushed
½ teaspoon ground red chili
1 teaspoon baharat (see Tip below)
1 teaspoon ground turmeric
1 cinnamon stick, about 1½ inches (4 cm) long
1 cup (6 oz/180 g) chopped, peeled tomatoes
2 dried limes or zest (rind) of ½ lemon
½ cup (4 fl oz/125 ml) water
steamed rice, for serving

Rinse fish and pat dry with paper towels. Cut into serving sizes and sprinkle lightly with salt. Place on a plate, cover and set aside.

In a wok over medium–low heat, heat ghee or oil. Add onion and cook until translucent, about 10 minutes. Add ginger, garlic, chili, baharat, turmeric and cinnamon stick and cook, stirring, for 2 minutes.

Add tomatoes, dried limes (pierced twice with a skewer) or lemon zest, and water. Add salt to taste, cover and simmer for 15 minutes.

Place fish pieces in sauce, cover and simmer until fish is cooked through, 15–20 minutes. Lift fish onto a platter with prepared rice. Remove dried lime or lemon zest and cinnamon stick from sauce and spoon sauce over fish. Serve hot.

Tip

Baharat is a blend of spices used in the Persian Gulf States and Iraq. It can be found in Middle Eastern markets, or you can mix your own by combining the following spices: 4 tablespoons each black pepper and mild paprika; 2 tablespoons each coriander seed, cassia cinnamon and cloves; 3 tablespoons cumin; and 1 teaspoon each cardamom and nutmeg. Store baharat in a tightly covered jar in a dark place for up to 6 months.

Fish fillets with coconut rice parcels and cilantro-tomato relish

Serves 4

2 tomatoes, chopped

¼ cup (⅓ oz/10 g) chopped cilantro (fresh coriander)

3 tablespoons lime juice

1 kaffir lime leaf, finely shredded

2 teaspoons peeled and grated ginger

¼ teaspoon ground coriander

pinch of ground turmeric

1 small white onion, finely chopped

1 green chili, seeded and chopped

2 tablespoons unsweetened dried (desiccated) shredded coconut

1 clove garlic, crushed

4 whole cloves

3–4 teaspoons lime juice

4 fish fillets such as perch or monk fish, 4–6 oz (125–180 g) each

¾ cup (5 oz/150 g) glutinous rice

1 tablespoon peanut oil

1 white onion, chopped

1 teaspoon ground cardamom

1 cup (8 fl oz/250 ml) water

½ cup (4 fl oz/125 ml) coconut milk

⅓ cup (3 fl oz/90 ml) warm water

4–6 fresh young banana leaves, rinsed and cut into 7-inch (18-cm) squares

In a bowl, combine tomatoes, cilantro, lime juice and kaffir lime leaves. Mix well and set aside.

In a small bowl, combine ginger, coriander, turmeric, onion, chili, coconut, garlic and cloves. Gradually add enough lime juice to form thick paste. If fish fillets have skin, slash skin side several times with sharp knife. Spread spice paste on flesh side of each fillet. Place on glass or ceramic plate, cover and refrigerate until ready to serve.

Place rice in fine-mesh sieve, rinse with cold running water and drain well.

In a wok over medium heat, warm peanut oil for 1 minute. Add onion and stir-fry until softened, about 2 minutes. Add rice, cardamom and water. Bring slowly to a boil, reduce heat to very low, cover tightly and cook until rice is tender, 12–14 minutes. Stir in coconut milk and warm water. Turn out on plate, leaving soft rice on bottom of wok. Allow to cool.

Working with one banana leaf square at a time, lay on work surface and spoon 2–3 tablespoons coconut rice in middle. Fold leaf over rice to form parcel. Secure with kitchen string.

Half fill large wok with water (steamer should not touch water) and bring to a boil. Working in batches if necessary, arrange parcels in bamboo steamer. Place each fish fillet on square of parchment (baking) paper and arrange fish in steamer. Cover, place steamer in a wok and steam until fish flakes when tested with fork, 6–8 minutes, depending on thickness of fillets. Remove fish and rice parcels from steamer and arrange on individual plates. Top each fish fillet with relish. Coconut rice parcels can be cut in half before serving, or guests can open parcels at table.

Fish with green curry paste

Serves 4

¼ cup (2 fl oz/60 ml) vegetable oil

¼ cup (2 fl oz/60 ml) green curry paste (see page 231)

12 oz (375 g) white fish fillets such as snapper, sole, or cod, thinly sliced

4 kaffir lime leaves, stemmed

1 cup (4 oz/125 g) chopped eggplant (aubergine) or 3 round Thai eggplants, chopped

½ cup (2 oz/60 g) pea eggplants (optional)

¼ cup (2 fl oz/60 ml) fish stock (see page 221) or water

1 fresh long red chili, coarsely chopped

1 cup (1 oz/30 g) loosely packed fresh sweet Thai basil leaves

⅓ cup (3 fl oz/90 ml) coconut cream plus 2 tablespoons, for garnish

1 tablespoon fish sauce

1 tablespoon soy sauce

1 tablespoon granulated (white) sugar

1 tablespoon palm sugar

In a wok or large, heavy frying pan, heat oil over medium–high heat. Add curry paste and fry, stirring constantly, until fragrant, 1–2 minutes. Add fish and gently stir until coated on all sides. Add kaffir lime leaves and eggplants. Cook for 1 minute, then add stock or water.

Bring just to a boil, stirring, then add chili, basil, ⅓ cup (3 fl oz/90 ml) coconut cream, fish sauce, soy sauce and sugars. Cook for 1–2 minutes to heat through. Transfer to a serving bowl, drizzle over the remaining 2 tablespoons coconut cream, and serve.

Tips

- This is delicious chilled as well as hot but when serving chilled, delete the coconut cream garnish.
- For pork with green curry paste, substitute an equal quantity pork shoulder, loin, or tenderloin for the fish. Slice thinly, and proceed as above. Lamb leg or loin also makes a delicious substitute.

Ginger fish in nori wrapper

Serves 4

¼ cup (2 fl oz/60 ml) shaoxing wine or dry sherry
¼ cup (2 fl oz/60 ml) light soy sauce
1 tablespoon fish sauce
1 teaspoon Asian sesame oil
4 fish fillets (snapper, bream, perch, salmon), about 6 oz (185 g) each, and 5–6 inches (12–15 cm) long
8 scallions (shallots/spring onions)
4 sheets toasted nori (yaki-nori or toasted seaweed)
½ red bell pepper (capsicum), seeded and thinly sliced
3 tablespoons Japanese pickled ginger

Mix wine, soy sauce, fish sauce and sesame oil in a bowl, and pour over fish fillets in a flat dish. Leave for 20–30 minutes, turning once. Drain, discarding marinade.

Cut scallions into same length as fish fillets, leaving some green top on. Lay each fillet diagonally across a sheet of nori. If nori is too big for fillets, trim to smaller square shape. Place 2 or 3 strips of bell pepper and slices of pickled ginger down center of fish fillet. Add 2 scallions, with one green tip and one white tip at each end. Lightly brush each side flap of nori with water and fold over fish towards center, pressing gently to seal. Fish and vegetable strips will still be visible at either end. Place 2 fish on each level of steamer, and cover.

Partially fill a large wok or pot with water (steamer should not touch water) and bring to a rapid simmer. Place steamer over water and steam until fish flakes when tested with fork and flesh is opaque, 5–8 minutes, depending on thickness of fillets. Switch steamer levels halfway through for even cooking. Remove fish from steamer and serve with remaining pickled ginger and steamed rice.

Lobster salad

Serves 6–8

1 cucumber

4 carrots

2 celery stalks, chopped into fine julienne

6 oz (180 g) pearl onions or small boiling (pickling) onions

1 tablespoon rice vinegar or distilled white vinegar

1 teaspoon sugar

1 tablespoon fish sauce

2 teaspoons salt

1 fresh long red chili, seeded and chopped

1½ cups (3 oz/90 g) fresh bean sprouts, rinsed and drained

1 lb (500 g) shelled meat from lobster tails or langoustines (scampi/saltwater crayfish)

1 tablespoon fish sauce

¼ teaspoon ground pepper

½ teaspoon chili powder or to taste

2 teaspoons finely chopped brown or pink shallots (French shallots)

½-inch (12 mm) piece fresh ginger, peeled and finely grated

For lime and chili dressing

1 teaspoon Asian sesame oil

2 teaspoons water

1 tablespoon fresh lime juice

½ teaspoon grated fresh ginger or ginger juice

¼ fresh long red chili, seeded and finely chopped

½ teaspoon salt

¼ teaspoon ground pepper

2 tablespoons coarsely chopped cilantro (fresh coriander) sprigs, for garnish

Cut cucumber lengthwise in half, then use a spoon to scoop out and discard seeds. Cut carrots and cucumber into strips the size of French fries. Plunge pearl onions into boiling water, then drain and slip off skins. If using small boiling onions, peel and quarter. In a medium bowl, combine vinegar, sugar, fish sauce, salt and chili. Add vegetables and sprouts and toss to coat. Let stand for 15–20 minutes.

Cut lobster meat into medallions about ½ inch (12 mm) thick. In a medium bowl, combine fish sauce, pepper, chili powder, shallots and ginger. Add lobster and toss to coat. Let stand for 10 minutes. In a large nonstick wok over medium–high heat, sauté lobster until opaque, about 2 minutes.

For lime and chili dressing: In a small bowl, combine sesame oil, water, lime juice, ginger, chili, salt and pepper. Add to lobster and toss to coat. To serve, drain marinated vegetables and arrange on a serving plate. Layer lobster medallions on top and sprinkle with cilantro.

Mussels with garlic and lime butter

Serves 4

2 lb (1 kg) mussels
½ cup (4 oz/125 g) butter, softened
2 cloves garlic, crushed
2 tablespoons chopped fresh parsley
2 tablespoons chopped fresh chives
1 teaspoon grated lime zest (rind)
freshly cracked black pepper to taste

Scrub mussels under cold running water with a nylon pad or stiff brush and pull off hair-like "beards", discarding any mussels that are cracked or do not close when tapped. Place in a large bamboo steamer or steamer basket. In a small bowl, mix butter, garlic, parsley, chives, lime zest and pepper.

Partially fill a large wok or pot with water (steamer should not touch water) and bring to a rapid simmer. Place steamer over water, cover, and steam until mussels open, 4–6 minutes. Remove from steamer, spoon butter mixture into each shell, and serve immediately with a tossed green salad and crusty bread.

Tips

- Substitute basil pesto for garlic and lime butter.
- Remove mussels from shells and place one or two on an endive (chicory/witloof) leaf, and serve topped with lime butter.
- Substitute shelled and deveined shrimp (prawns) for mussels.

Pad thai with shrimp

Serves 4

5 oz (150 g) thick rice stick noodles

5 tablespoons vegetable oil

4 oz (125 g) firm tofu, cut into 1-inch (2.5-cm) cubes

2 cloves garlic, crushed

1 lb (500 g) jumbo shrimp (king prawns), peeled and
  deveined, tails intact

3 tablespoons lemon juice

2 tablespoons fish sauce

3 tablespoons palm sugar or brown sugar

2 eggs, beaten

2 tablespoons chopped chives

2 tablespoons chopped cilantro (fresh coriander)

2 tablespoons chopped fresh basil

2 tablespoons fried onion

lemon wedges for serving

Cook noodles, then drain and set aside. In a wok or frying pan, heat oil over medium–high heat. Add tofu and cook, stirring constantly, until golden, 1–2 minutes. Drain on paper towels. Drain all but 2 tablespoons oil from pan and return to medium–high heat. Add garlic and shrimp and cook, stirring occasionally, until shrimp change color, 4–5 minutes. Add lemon juice, fish sauce and sugar, stirring until sugar dissolves. Mix in noodles.

Push noodle mixture to one side of wok or pan. Add eggs and cook, without stirring, until partially set. Then stir gently until scrambled. Stir egg through noodle mixture. Add tofu, chives, cilantro and basil. Cook until heated through, about 1 minute.

To serve, divide among individual plates and sprinkle with fried onion. Accompany with lemon wedges.

Sautéed squid with leeks

Serves 6

1 lb (500 g) cleaned squid (calamari)
  (see Tips below)
3 tablespoons fish sauce
½ teaspoon ground pepper
2 large leeks or 6 baby leeks, white part only, well
  rinsed
4 scallions (shallots/spring onions), including green
  parts, chopped
3 tablespoons vegetable oil
3 small tomatoes, quartered or sectioned
1 onion, coarsely chopped
⅓-inch (1-cm) knob fresh ginger, peeled and cut
  into fine julienne
1 tablespoon cornstarch (cornflour) or arrowroot
  dissolved in 1 tablespoon water
steamed rice, for serving

Marinate squid (calamari) in 2 tablespoons fish sauce and pepper.

Cut leeks and scallions into fine julienne.

In a wok, heat oil over high heat and sauté squid for 1 minute. Add leeks, tomatoes, onion, ginger and scallions. Stir-fry for 2 minutes, then add cornstarch and water mixture. Stir well, then reduce heat to low, cover, and simmer for 3 minutes. Stir in remaining 1 tablespoon fish sauce. Serve hot with steamed rice.

Tips

- Do not overcook squid as it becomes tough and rubbery.
- If using uncleaned squid, increase proportion accordingly. To clean, pull tentacles and head from the tubelike body. Cut directly behind eyes to free tentacles from eyes. Use two fingers to pull out plastic-like cartilage and innards, and discard. Rinse and reserve tentacles and tubes. If small, cut squid bodies in half or quarters, and larger squid into 1-x-2-inch (2.5-x-5-cm) pieces.
- To tenderize and beautify larger squid, lightly score inside of flesh with a sharp knife, making a lattice pattern. This works best with larger bodies, as small squid are thin.

Scallops with arugula pesto and sweet potato purée

Serves 4

1 bunch arugula (rocket)

¼ cup (1 oz/30 g) pine nuts, toasted

¼ cup (1 oz/30 g) grated parmesan cheese

ground pepper to taste

2 cloves garlic, crushed

¼ cup (2 fl oz/60 ml) extra virgin olive oil

1 lb (500 g) sweet potatoes, peeled and cut
   into 2-inch (5-cm) pieces

2 tablespoons olive oil

3 cloves garlic, crushed

2 tablespoons vegetable oil

1 small red chili, seeded and chopped

1 lb (500 g) scallops, halved if large

1 tablespoon lime juice

lime wedges for serving

Place arugula, pine nuts, parmesan cheese, pepper and garlic in food processor. Process until finely chopped. With motor running, gradually pour in olive oil and process until well combined. Set aside.

Half fill saucepan with water. Bring to a boil, add sweet potatoes, reduce heat to medium and cook until tender, 10–12 minutes. Drain, transfer to bowl and mash with fork or potato masher. Stir in olive oil and 2 garlic cloves. Set aside and keep warm.

In a wok over medium heat, warm vegetable oil. Add chili and remaining garlic clove and stir-fry until aromatic, about 1 minute. Add scallops and stir-fry until tender (do not overcook or scallops will toughen), 2–3 minutes. Remove from heat and stir in lime juice.

To serve, spoon sweet potato purée on individual plates. Top with pesto, then place scallops over pesto. Serve hot, accompanied with lime wedges. Store any leftover pesto in screw-top jar in refrigerator.

Seafood, basil and almond stir-fried with mixed greens

Serves 4

1 lb (500 g) medium uncooked shrimp (prawns)

¼ cup (2 fl oz/60 ml) vegetable oil

2 cloves garlic, minced

1 large hot red chili, finely chopped

4 oz (125 g) slivered almonds, toasted

2 tablespoons oyster sauce

2 tablespoons soy sauce

8 scallions (shallots/spring onions), chopped

3 bunches (about 1½ lb/650 g) baby bok choy, chopped

4 oz (125 g) snow peas (mange tout), sliced diagonally

1 handful shredded basil leaves

cooked rice or noodles, to serve

Remove head and shells from shrimp, leaving tails intact. Heat oil in wok or large frying pan until just smoking.

Add shrimp and stir-fry 2 minutes or until they start to change color.

Add garlic, chili, almonds, sauces and scallions and stir-fry 2–3 minutes or until fragrant and onions are tender.

Stir in bok choy and snow peas and cook, stirring, 2 minutes or until just tender. Stir in basil and serve with rice or noodles.

Semolina-crusted shrimp

Serves 4–5

¼ cup coriander seeds

1–2 tablespoons vegetable oil

4 teaspoons finely grated fresh ginger

4 teaspoons crushed garlic

4 teaspoons tamarind concentrate

2–4 teaspoons chili powder

2 teaspoons fennel seeds

1 teaspoon ground turmeric

18 fresh curry leaves, finely chopped

salt to taste

2 lb (1 kg) medium shrimp (prawns), peeled
  and deveined

vegetable oil for deep-frying

1 cup (6 oz/180 g) coarse semolina

juice of 1 lemon

In a spice grinder, grind coriander seeds to a powder. Place in a bowl and combine with 1–2 tablespoons oil, ginger, garlic, tamarind, chili powder, fennel seeds, turmeric, curry leaves and salt to form a paste.

Add shrimp to spice paste and mix well until coated. Set aside to marinate for 5 minutes.

Fill a karhai or wok with vegetable oil to a depth of 2 inches (5 cm) and heat over medium heat to 375°F (190°C) on a deep-frying thermometer. While oil is heating, dip shrimp, one at a time, in semolina to coat. Fry shrimp in batches until light golden, 1–2 minutes. Use a slotted spoon to remove shrimp to paper towels to drain.

Drizzle shrimp with lemon juice and serve hot.

Spiced shrimp and rice

Serves 4–5

2–3 tablespoons ghee or vegetable oil

2 cloves garlic, chopped

2 lb (1 kg) raw shrimp (prawns), shelled and deveined

1 large yellow (brown) onion, chopped

2 teaspoons baharat (page 120)

2 teaspoons turmeric

1½ cups (9 oz/280 g) chopped, peeled tomatoes

2 teaspoons salt

freshly ground black pepper

1 tablespoon chopped fresh flat-leaf (Italian) parsley

1 teaspoon chopped cilantro (fresh coriander)

2½ cups (20 fl oz/625 ml) water

2 cups (14 oz/440 g) basmati rice

In a large pot over high heat, heat 1 tablespoon ghee. Add garlic and shrimp and cook, stirring frequently, until shrimp turn pink. Remove shrimp to a plate and set aside.

Add remaining ghee to the pot and heat over medium–low heat. Add onion and cook until translucent and lightly browned, about 8 minutes. Stir in Baharat and turmeric and cook for 1 minute.

Add tomatoes, salt, pepper to taste, parsley and cilantro. Bring to a boil and add water. Cover and cook over medium heat for 5 minutes.

Place rice in a fine-mesh sieve and rinse under cold running water until water runs clear. Stir into sauce and bring to a boil. Reduce heat to low, cover and cook for 18 minutes.

Stir rice, then put shrimp on top of rice and gently stir through rice. Cover pot and simmer over low heat for 3 minutes.

Stir rice again then leave covered, off the heat, for 5 minutes. Serve with pita bread, pickles and salad.

Spicy snapper with parsnip chips

Serves 4

2 teaspoon ground cumin

1 green chili, seeded and sliced

½ cup (⅔ oz/20 g) cilantro (fresh coriander) leaves

3 cloves garlic

1 piece peeled fresh ginger, about 1¼ in (3 cm)

2 teaspoons garam marsala (see page 225)

4 small snapper, 6–8 oz (180–250 g) each, cleaned

6 cups (48 fl oz/1.5 L) vegetable oil for deep-frying

2 parsnips, peeled

lime wedges for serving

Place cumin, chili, cilantro, garlic, ginger and garam marsala in food processor and process until smooth. Using sharp knife, cut 3 shallow slits in each side of fish. Rub spice mixture into each side. Place on glass or ceramic plate, cover and refrigerate for 1 hour.

Heat vegetable oil in a wok until it reaches 375°F (190°C) on a deep-frying thermometer or until a small bread cube dropped in oil sizzles and turns golden. Add fish, one at a time, and cook, turning once, until golden and crisp on both sides, about 4 minutes. Using tongs and spatula, carefully remove fish from wok and drain on paper towels. Repeat with remaining fish. Keep warm.

Thinly slice parsnips lengthwise, using vegetable peeler. Add slices to wok and cook until golden and crisp, about 1 minute. Using slotted spoon, remove from wok and drain on paper towels.

Arrange fish and parsnip chips on individual plates. Garnish with lime wedge and serve.

Squid bulgogi

Serves 4

3 medium squid tubes (bodies), about 6½ oz (200 g)
   total, cut open and cleaned
4 fresh shiitake mushrooms or dried Chinese
   mushrooms soaked for 30 minutes in several
   changes of water
2 small green bell peppers (capsicums), cut into
   bite-sized pieces
2 tablespoons vegetable or sunflower oil
lettuce leaves, for serving
1 teaspoon pan-toasted sesame seeds
1 teaspoon freshly ground black pepper
1 teaspoon thin hot red chili strips

For marinade
3 tablespoons light soy sauce
2 tablespoons sugar
2 tablespoons crushed garlic
2 scallions (shallots/spring onions), finely chopped
1 teaspoon ginger juice (obtained by grating fresh
   ginger)
1 teaspoon sesame oil
steamed rice, for serving

Using the tip of a knife, score surface of squid in a
crisscross pattern to prevent it over-curling during cooking.
Cut squid into bite-sized pieces.

If using fresh shiitake mushrooms, dip in rapidly boiling
water for a few seconds. Remove and drain on paper
towels, then chop roughly. If using dried mushrooms,
squeeze out excess water. Remove and discard stems and
roughly chop caps.

To make marinade: In a small bowl, combine marinade
ingredients and mix well.

In a large glass or ceramic bowl, combine squid,
mushrooms and bell peppers with marinade and marinate
for 20–30 minutes.

In a wok or frying pan, heat oil until very hot. Drain squid,
mushroom and bell pepper pieces and cook over high heat
until liquid has evaporated and marinade has caramelized,
about 5 minutes.

Arrange lettuce leaves on individual plates and place squid
bulgogi in center. Sprinkle with sesame seeds, black
pepper and chili strips, and serve with steamed rice.

Steamed fish in banana leaves

Makes 8–10

1 tablespoon sticky (glutinous) rice

¼ cup (2 fl oz/60 ml) vegetable oil

¼ cup (2 fl oz/60 ml) red curry paste (see page 231)

½ cup (2 oz/60 g) chopped eggplant (aubergine)

¼ cup (1 oz/30 g) pea eggplants (optional)

4 long beans or 12 green beans, cut into
    ½-inch (12-mm) pieces

¼ cup (2 fl oz/60 ml) chicken stock (see page 220)
    or water

2 tablespoons fish sauce

8 fresh eryngo (sawtooth coriander) leaves, finely
    shredded, or 7 sprigs cilantro (fresh coriander),
    coarsely chopped

12 oz (375 g) firm white-fleshed fish fillets such as cod,
    skinned and very thinly sliced

4 kaffir lime leaves, stemmed

1–2 large banana leaves (optional)

about 10 fresh piper (beetle) leaves, or 2–3 cabbage
    leaves, each cut into 4 squares

In a wok or small frying pan over low heat, stir rice until golden brown, 3–5 minutes. Transfer to a mortar and pulverize with a pestle; set aside.

In a wok or large, heavy frying pan, warm oil over medium–high heat and fry curry paste, stirring constantly, until fragrant, 1–2 minutes. Add eggplants and beans and stir well to coat. Add chicken stock or water, fish sauce, and eryngo leaves or cilantro, and bring to a boil. Add fish, stirring to coat well, then add ground rice and cook until mixture is very thick and fish is just opaque throughout, about 1 minute. Remove from heat.

Roll kaffir lime leaves together into a tight cylinder and cut into fine shreds. If using, wipe banana leaf with a clean cloth. Spread out each banana leaf and cut each into 8–10 pieces, 8 x 6 inches (20 x 15 cm) in size, removing hard center stem. Center a piper leaf on each piece of banana leaf (or alternatively, cut each cabbage leaf into 8–10 small squares and place 1 square on each banana leaf) and spoon about ¼ cup fish mixture on top. Sprinkle strands of shredded lime leaf over. Gently roll over sides of banana leaf, overlapping them to make a shape resembling a flat sausage. Fold or pull over 2 opposite ends to center, and secure with a toothpick. Cook parcels in covered steamer over rapidly simmering water for about 15 minutes. Let cool slightly, then open parcels and serve on banana leaves.

Tips

- This dish is ideal for picnics or at a buffet, as it is delicious eaten at room temperature.
- Lay banana leaves in the sun for a couple of hours to soften slightly so they are easier to fold. Or, run them briefly over a gas flame until they become waxy and pliable. Very fresh leaves, especially young tender ones, are best. Alternatively, use aluminum foil.
- If available, you can also add 1 teaspoon prickly ash (kamchatton), coarsely ground, to the ground rice.

Stir-fried chili-lime shrimp

Serves 4

1 lb (500 g) jumbo shrimp (king prawns), peeled
   and deveined, tails intact
pinch of ground chili
¼ teaspoon ground turmeric
3 tablespoons vegetable oil
3 cloves garlic, crushed
1 small red chili, seeded and chopped
1 teaspoon black mustard seeds
1 tablespoon lime juice
lime wedges for serving

Place shrimp in bowl. Combine ground chili and turmeric and sprinkle over shrimp. Using hands, rub spices into shrimp.

In a wok over medium–high heat, warm vegetable oil. Add garlic, chili and mustard seeds and stir-fry until seeds begin to pop, 1–2 minutes. Raise heat to high, add shrimp and stir-fry until shrimp change color and are tender, 3–4 minutes. Remove from heat and stir in lime juice.

Serve hot, accompanied with lime wedges.

Stir-fried octopus with long beans and snow peas

Serves 4

1 lb (500 g) baby octopus

1 tablespoon light soy sauce

3 tablespoons vegetable oil

1 tablespoon dry sherry

2 cloves garlic, crushed

2 teaspoons grated lime zest (rind)

2 tablespoons lime juice

3 small red chilies, seeded and halved lengthwise

5 oz (150 g) long beans, cut into 4-inch (10-cm) lengths

4 kaffir lime leaves, shredded, or 1 teaspoon grated lime zest (rind)

5 oz (150 g) snow peas (mange-tout), trimmed and sliced crosswise

Working with one octopus at a time, slit open head and remove intestines. Rinse and place in glass or ceramic bowl. In small bowl, combine soy sauce, 1 tablespoon vegetable oil, sherry, garlic, 2 teaspoons lime zest and lime juice. Pour over octopus, cover and refrigerate for 1 hour.

Drain octopus and reserve marinade. In a wok over medium heat, warm remaining 2 tablespoons vegetable oil. Add chilies and stir-fry until aromatic, 1–2 minutes. Add octopus and stir-fry for 2 minutes. Add beans, lime leaves or lime zest, snow peas and reserved marinade. Stir-fry until vegetables are tender-crisp and octopus is cooked through (do not overcook or octopus will toughen), 1–2 minutes.

Serve hot.

Tip

You may like to substitute octopus with six 1-lb (500-g) squid bodies. Cut squid tubes in half lengthwise. Cut shallow slashes in a criss-cross pattern on outside of squid and cut squid into 3/4-inch (2-cm) strips. Marinate and cook as for octopus.

Stir-fried seafood with noodles

Serves 4

8 oz (250 g) soft Asian noodles

1 tablespoon peanut oil

2 teaspoons sesame oil

1 tablespoon chopped lemongrass

3 cloves garlic, chopped

1 red chili, seeded and chopped

8 oz (250 g) uncooked shrimp (prawns), peeled
   and deveined

8 oz (250 g) fish fillets, skinned and cut into
   small pieces

8 oz (250 g) scallops, deveined if necessary

2 tablespoons fish sauce

2 tablespoons chopped cilantro (fresh coriander) leaves

1 tablespoon sweet chili sauce

Cook noodles in boiling salted water for 5 minutes. Drain.

In a wok over medium heat, warm peanut and sesame oils. Add lemongrass, garlic and chili and cook until fragrant, about 1 minute. Add shrimp and fish and cook until tender and opaque, 3–5 minutes. Stir in noodles, scallops, fish sauce, cilantro and chili sauce and cook, stirring well, until noodles are heated through and scallops are tender, about 3–4 minutes. Serve immediately.

Stir-fried squid with chili

Makes 4 small servings

4 cleaned squid tubes, about 12 oz (375 g) total
2 tablespoons vegetable oil
1 teaspoon Asian sesame oil
3 cloves garlic, finely chopped
1–2 small red chilies, seeded and finely chopped

Cut squid in half lengthwise, then cut into strips ¾-inch (2-cm) wide. In a wok or frying pan, warm oils over medium heat. Fry garlic and chili until aromatic, about 1 minute. Add squid and stir-fry for 1 minute. Do not overcook or squid will become tough. Remove from heat and serve hot.

Thai curry fish in banana leaf cups

Serves 6

2–3 large banana leaves, cut into six 6-inch (15-cm)
    rounds
1 lb (500 g) white fish fillets, finely diced
2 tablespoons red curry paste (see page 231)
1 tablespoon chopped roasted peanuts
1 cup (8 oz/250 ml) thick coconut cream
2 eggs, lightly beaten
1 tablespoon fish sauce
salt and pepper to taste
1 cup (3 oz/90 g) Chinese cabbage leaves, finely
    shredded
2 tablespoons thick coconut cream, for garnish
    (optional)
1 fresh long red chili, seeded and thinly sliced,
    for garnish (optional)

Drop each banana leaf round into hot water to soften, 30–60 seconds. Drain and pat dry with paper towels. Fold each round and staple into a round or square custard cup, or use rounds to line oiled rice bowls or ramekins.

Partially fill a wok or pot with water (steamer should not touch water) and bring to a rapid simmer. In a bowl, combine fish, curry paste, peanuts, coconut cream, eggs, fish sauce, salt and pepper. Fill each banana cup with ⅙ fish mixture, then ⅙ shredded cabbage, and place in a bamboo steamer or steamer basket. Cover with double layer of greased plastic wrap or parchment (baking) paper, or place a cloth under lid to stop any condensation dripping onto cups. Place steamer over water, cover, and steam until set, 10–15 minutes. Garnish with a dollop of coconut cream and sliced chili if desired. Serve hot.

Thai red curry shrimp

Serves 4

1½ lb (750 g) jumbo shrimp (king prawns), with heads
1 tablespoon vegetable oil
2 tablespoons red curry paste (see page 231)
2 cups (16 fl oz/500 ml) coconut milk
1 tablespoon fish sauce
1 fresh red Thai or Anaheim chili, seeded and cut into
    shreds 2 inches (5 cm) long, for garnish

Shell and devein shrimp, leaving tails intact and reserving shrimp heads. Wash shrimp heads. In a wok or large skillet, heat oil over medium heat and fry shrimp heads until they turn pink, about 1 minute. Add curry paste and fry until fragrant, about 30 seconds. Add coconut milk and fish sauce. Reduce heat to low and simmer for 10 minutes. Using a slotted spoon, remove and discard shrimp heads. Add shrimp to curry and stir over low heat until shrimp turn pink, 4–5 minutes. Spoon into serving bowls. Garnish each serving with shredded red chili. Serve with steamed jasmine rice.

Whole fried fish with chili and basil

Serves 4

1–2 whole fish, about 9½ inches (24 cm) long,
   such as snapper, bream, flounder or trout,
   scaled and gutted

vegetable oil, for deep-frying, plus 2 tablespoons

6 cloves garlic, coarsely chopped

1 onion, finely chopped

5 fresh medium-sized red chilies, thinly sliced

1 fresh long red chili, cut into large pieces

1 fresh long green chili, cut into large pieces

1 tablespoon fish sauce

1 tablespoon soy sauce

¼ cup (2 fl oz/60 ml) chicken stock (see page 220)
   or water

¾ cup (¾ oz/20 g) loosely packed sweet Thai basil
   leaves, coarsely chopped

½ cup (¾ oz/20 g) chopped cilantro (fresh coriander)
   leaves

With a very sharp knife, score each side of fish with three deep slashes to the bone.

In a large wok or deep-fryer, heat 4 inches (10 cm) oil to 350°F (180°C). Add fish and cook until crispy and brown on both sides and opaque throughout, 7–10 minutes, depending on thickness. Using a skimmer, transfer fish to paper towels to drain.

Meanwhile, in a wok or medium-sized heavy frying pan over medium–high heat, heat 2 tablespoons oil and fry garlic, onion, and all chilies until garlic just begins to brown. Add fish sauce, soy sauce and chicken stock or water, stir to combine, then cook for 1 minute. Add basil leaves, stir well and pour over fish. Transfer to a large serving platter, sprinkle with chopped cilantro, and serve.

Tips

- For a less piquant dish, remove seeds from chilies.
- This dish can also be garnished with fried basil leaves. In a large wok, heat 1 cup (8 fl oz/250 ml) oil. Working in batches, fry about 20 fresh basil leaves. Using a slotted spoon, remove from oil and drain on paper towels.

vegetables and salads

Asian greens stir-fry with shiitake mushroom

Serves 4

1 lb (500 g) Asian greens, such as bok choy,
   choy sum or Chinese cabbage
2 tablespoons vegetable oil
1 red bell pepper (capsicum), seeded and sliced
   into strips
1 small red chili, seeded and sliced
10 scallions (shallots/spring onions), trimmed
   and sliced
2 celery stalks, sliced
1 lemongrass stalk, trimmed and chopped
2 cloves garlic, crushed
1 inch (2.5 cm) piece fresh ginger, peeled and chopped
6 oz (180 g) shiitake mushrooms, sliced
3 tablespoons soy sauce
cooked egg noodles or jasmine rice, for serving

Wash Asian greens well and pat dry with paper towels. Trim off root ends and slice greens into 2½-inch (6-cm) lengths.

In a wok or large frying pan, heat oil over medium heat, until oil is hot but not smoking. Add bell pepper, chili, scallions, celery, lemongrass, garlic and ginger. Raise heat to medium-high and stir-fry for 2 minutes. Add greens and mushrooms and stir-fry for 2 minutes. Reduce heat to low, cover and allow mixture to cook slowly until greens are tender–crisp, about 2 minutes. Remove from heat and stir in soy sauce.

Serve immediately with egg noodles or jasmine rice.

Asian greens with lemon and ginger oil

Serves 4

⅓ cup (3 fl oz/90 ml) sunflower oil

finely grated zest (rind) of 2 lemons

1 lemongrass stalk, bottom 3 inches (7.5 cm) only,
  inner stalks roughly chopped

3 teaspoons peeled and grated fresh ginger

1 lb (500 g) mixed Asian greens, such as bok choy,
  choy sum and Chinese cabbage

pinch sea salt

pinch sugar

juice of 1 lemon

lemon wedges, for serving

Place oil, lemon zest, lemongrass and ginger in a screw-top jar and shake until well combined. Set aside in a warm place for 5 days so flavors infuse oil. After 5 days, strain oil and discard solids. Seal and store lemon and ginger oil in a cool, dark place.

Wash greens well. Pat dry with paper towels. Trim roots from greens and cut into 2-inch (5-cm) lengths. If using bok choy, remove dark outer leaves, separate younger leaves and trim ends.

Warm 2 tablespoons lemon and ginger oil in a wok or frying pan over medium heat. Add greens and stir-fry until tender-crisp, 3 to 4 minutes. Remove from heat and stir in salt, sugar and lemon juice.

Serve immediately, accompanied with lemon wedges.

Asian greens with tempeh and oyster sauce

Serves 2–4

1 bunch bok choy or choy sum, trimmed and
　　cut into 4-inch (10-cm) lengths

3 oz (90 g) tempeh or tofu (bean curd), cut
　　into ½-inch (12-mm) pieces

3 oz (90 g) enoki mushrooms, trimmed

3½ oz (100 g) bottled baby corn, halved

¼ cup (2 fl oz/60 ml) oyster sauce

1 clove garlic, crushed

1 teaspoon Asian sesame oil

½ teaspoon peeled and grated fresh ginger

2 scallions (shallots/spring onions), finely chopped

1 tablespoon sesame seeds, toasted

Put bok choy, tempeh, enoki and baby corn in a large bamboo steamer or steamer basket. Partially fill a wok or pot with water (steamer should not touch water) and bring to a rapid simmer. Put steamer over water, cover, and steam until vegetables are softened, 3–4 minutes.

Meanwhile, put oyster sauce, garlic, sesame oil, and ginger in a small saucepan and mix well. Place saucepan over medium heat to warm sauce, 3–4 minutes.

Remove vegetables from steamer and arrange on serving plates with enoki in the center. Drizzle warm sauce over vegetables. Sprinkle with scallions and sesame seeds. Serve as a side dish or light vegetarian dish.

Beans foogarth

Serves 4

2 lb (1 kg) green beans, trimmed and cut
   into ½-inch (12-mm) pieces

1½ teaspoons ground turmeric

2½ tablespoons vegetable oil

1 teaspoon brown or black mustard seeds

5 dried red chilies

18 fresh curry leaves

1 tablespoon finely grated fresh ginger

2 yellow (brown) onions, chopped

½ teaspoon salt

4 fresh green chilies, chopped

½ cup (2 oz/60 g) finely grated fresh coconut

juice of ½ lemon

Fill a saucepan with water and bring to a boil. Add beans and ½ teaspoon turmeric and boil for 1–2 minutes. Drain and rinse beans under cold running water. Drain well.

In a karhai or wok, heat oil over medium–low heat. Add mustard seeds and cook until they crackle, about 30 seconds. Add dried chilies, curry leaves and ginger, and cook, stirring, for 30 seconds. Add onions, remaining 1 teaspoon turmeric and salt. Cook, uncovered, stirring often, until onions are translucent, about 5 minutes.

Stir in beans and fresh chilies, and toss over medium– low heat until well combined and heated through. Sprinkle with coconut and drizzle with lemon juice. Serve hot.

Tip

The addition of turmeric when cooking beans helps to intensify the green color of the beans.

Black-eyed pea and sugar snaps stir-fry

Serves 4

1 cup (6½ oz/200 g) dried black-eyed peas (beans)

2 red onions, sliced

juice from 2 lemons

1 tablespoon vegetable oil

2 teaspoons Asian sesame oil

5 oz (150 g) sugar snap peas or snow peas
  (mange-tout), trimmed

½ cup (2 oz/60 g) chopped scallions (shallots/spring
  onions)

1 cup (1 oz/30 g) mint leaves

½ cup (¾ oz/20 g) snipped chives

1 teaspoon fish sauce

1 teaspoon light soy sauce

Place black-eyed peas in large bowl, add cold water to cover, cover and allow to stand overnight. Drain and rinse peas and place in saucepan with plenty of water to cover. Bring to a boil, reduce heat to low and simmer, uncovered, until tender, about 1 hour. Drain and allow to cool completely.

In bowl, combine onions and lemon juice, cover and allow to stand for 1 hour.

In wok over medium-high heat, warm vegetable and sesame oils. Add sugar snap peas or snow peas and stir-fry until tender-crisp, about 2 minutes. Remove from heat and allow to cool completely. Add black-eyed peas and sugar snap peas or snow peas to bowl with onions. Add scallions, mint, chives, fish sauce and soy sauce. Mix well, cover and refrigerate for 30 minutes. Serve chilled.

Butternut squash and lentil salad

Serves 4

⅓ cup (3 fl oz/90 ml) olive oil

2 teaspoons grated lime zest (rind)

⅓ cup (3 fl oz/90 ml) lime juice

2 tablespoons chopped cilantro (fresh coriander)

½ teaspoon superfine (caster) sugar

ground pepper to taste

1 butternut squash (pumpkin), about 1 lb (500 g),
   peeled and cut into 1½-in (4-cm) cubes

½ cup (3½ oz/100 g) dried red lentils

1 tablespoon vegetable oil

1 small red chili, seeded and chopped

1 teaspoon cumin seeds

2 teaspoons coriander seeds, cracked

Place olive oil, lime zest and juice, cilantro, sugar and pepper in screw-top jar. Shake well to combine. Set aside

Line large steamer with parchment (baking) paper. Half fill wok with water (steamer should not touch water) and bring to a boil. Place squash cubes in steamer, cover and place steamer over boiling water. Steam until squash cubes are tender but retain their shape, 10–12 minutes. Add more water to wok when necessary. Remove steamer from wok and let squash cool.

Place lentils in saucepan with water to cover. Bring to a boil and cook until tender (do not overcook), about 5 minutes. Drain and cool.

In wok over medium–high heat, warm vegetable oil. Add chili, cumin and coriander and cook until aromatic, 1–2 minutes. Add squash and lentils and stir-fry until flavors are blended, about 1 minute. Remove from heat and stir in dressing. Mix well.

Serve warm or refrigerate for 30 minutes and serve chilled.

Chickpeas with spinach

Serves 6

1½ cups (10 oz/300 g) dried chickpeas (garbanzo beans)

4 cups (32 fl oz/1 L) cold water

⅓ cup (3 fl oz/90 ml) olive oil

1 large yellow (brown) onion, chopped

2 cloves garlic, chopped

¼ cup (2 oz/60 g) tomato paste

2 tablespoons chopped fresh flat-leaf (Italian) parsley

1 tablespoon chopped fresh mint

1 teaspoon ground cumin

1 teaspoon sugar

salt

freshly ground black pepper

1½ lb (750 g) spinach

extra-virgin olive oil, for serving

Put chickpeas in a bowl, add water and let soak in a cool place for 8–10 hours or overnight.

Drain chickpeas and rinse well. Place in a large saucepan with fresh water to cover. Bring to a boil, cover and cook over low heat until tender, 1–1½ hours.

Heat oil in a wok over medium–low heat. Add onion and cook until translucent, about 7 minutes. Add garlic and cook for a few seconds. Stir in tomato paste, parsley, mint, cumin, sugar and salt and black pepper to taste. Add to chickpeas, cover and simmer for 10 minutes.

Remove any attached roots and damaged leaves from spinach and discard. Wash spinach leaves and stems well in several changes of water. Drain, then coarsely chop leaves and stems. Add to chickpeas, stir well and simmer, uncovered, until spinach is cooked, about 10 minutes. Mixture should be moist, but not too liquid.

Serve hot or at room temperature. Add extra-virgin olive oil to taste.

Deep-fried tofu with vegetables

Serves 4

13 oz (400 g) firm tofu, drained and pressed
canola oil for deep-frying
3 tablespoons vegetable or chicken stock
3 tablespoons mirin or sweet white wine
2 tablespoons Japanese soy sauce
¼ teaspoon sugar
½ teaspoon Asian sesame oil
½ teaspoon grated fresh ginger
1 large carrot, julienned
½ small green bell pepper (capsicum), seeded
and julienned
½ small red bell pepper (capsicum), seeded and
julienned
1 medium red (Spanish) onion, cut into thin wedges
watercress sprigs for garnish

Cut tofu into 1½-inch (3-cm) cubes and pat dry with paper towels. Fill a large wok one-third full with oil and heat to 365°F (185°C). Deep-fry tofu until golden, 3–4 minutes, turning occasionally. Drain on paper towels. In a medium saucepan, combine stock, mirin, soy sauce, sugar, sesame oil and ginger. Bring to a boil, add vegetables and simmer 1 minute. Combine tofu with vegetables and sauce. Garnish with watercress and serve immediately.

Fried tofu salad

Serves 4

8 oz (250 g) egg noodles
1 English (hothouse) cucumber, thinly sliced
1 red bell pepper (capsicum), seeded and sliced
1 cup (4 oz/125 g) fresh bean sprouts, rinsed
3 tablespoons sliced scallions (shallots/spring onions)
2 tablespoons sesame seeds, toasted
3 tablespoons vegetable oil
6½ oz (200 g) firm tofu, cut into 1-inch (2.5-cm) cubes
2 cloves garlic
1-inch (2.5-cm) piece fresh ginger, peeled
6 tablespoons crunchy peanut butter
1 tablespoon Asian sesame oil
3 tablespoons rice wine
1 tablespoon Worcestershire sauce
3 teaspoons palm sugar or brown sugar
5 tablespoons chicken stock (see page 220)

Cook noodles, then drain and let cool.

In large bowl, combine cucumber, bell pepper, bean sprouts, scallions and sesame seeds. Cover and chill.

In wok or frying pan, heat oil over medium–high heat. Add tofu and cook, stirring constantly, until golden, 3–4 minutes. Drain on paper towels and let cool.

Add tofu and noodles to bowl. Add dressing and toss until well combined.

Place garlic, ginger, peanut butter, sesame oil, rice wine, Worcestershire sauce, sugar and stock in food processor. Process 10 seconds to make dressing.

Cover salad and refrigerate for 30 minutes.

To serve, divide chilled salad among individual plates and pour over dressing.

Green beans in oil

Serves 6

1 lb (500 g) green beans

¼ cup (2 fl oz/60 ml) olive oil

1 medium yellow (brown) onion, chopped

2 cloves garlic, chopped

1 cup (6 oz/185 g) chopped, peeled tomatoes

1 tablespoon tomato paste

½ cup (4 fl oz/125 ml) water

½ teaspoon sugar

salt

freshly ground black pepper

2 tablespoons chopped fresh flat-leaf (Italian) parsley

Trim beans and remove strings if necessary. Cut into 2-inch (5-cm) lengths or slit lengthwise.

Heat olive oil in a wok over medium–low heat. Add onion and fry until translucent, about 8 minutes. Add garlic and cook for a few seconds longer.

Add tomatoes, tomato paste, water, sugar and salt and pepper to taste. Cover and simmer until tomatoes are soft, about 15 minutes.

Add beans and parsley; cover and simmer until beans are tender, 15–20 minutes. Serve hot, or at room temperature as is traditional.

Homemade cottage cheese with spinach

Serves 4

2 bunches spinach, trimmed and rinsed well

1½ teaspoons ground turmeric

2 tablespoons water

3 tablespoons vegetable oil and melted unsalted
   butter combined

4 teaspoons cumin seeds

3 yellow (brown) onions, chopped

½ teaspoon salt

2 tablespoons coriander seeds, crushed

1½ tablespoons grated fresh ginger

2 fresh green chilies, finely chopped

1 teaspoon chili powder

3 tomatoes, unpeeled, finely chopped

1 recipe paneer (see page 229), cut into
   1-inch (2.5-cm) pieces

1 teaspoon dried fenugreek leaves

Place spinach in a large saucepan. In a small bowl, combine ½ teaspoon turmeric with water and add to pan. Cook over medium–high heat, covered, turning spinach occasionally, until spinach is wilted, 3–5 minutes. Remove from heat, drain excess water and let spinach cool. Place spinach in a food processor or blender and purée. Set aside.

In a wok, heat oil and butter mixture over medium–low heat. Add cumin seeds and cook until fragrant, about 30 seconds. Add onions and salt, and cook uncovered, stirring often, until onions are translucent, about 5 minutes.

Add coriander seeds, ginger, chilies, chili powder and remaining 1 teaspoon turmeric, and cook, stirring, until fragrant, 2–3 minutes.

Stir in tomatoes and cook, stirring occasionally, until tomatoes are soft, about 5 minutes. Stir in puréed spinach and mix well. Add paneer and stir gently to coat with sauce. Cook over medium–low heat until paneer is warmed through, 2–3 minutes. Sprinkle with fenugreek leaves and serve hot.

Tip
Adding ground turmeric to spinach before cooking helps spinach to retain a bright green color.

Japanese seaweed salad

Serves 4

1½ oz (40 g) hijiki

4 sheets usuage

boiling water

3 tablespoons vegetable oil

½ carrot, peeled and cut into thin matchstick strips

1 teaspoon instant dashi dissolved in

   1 cup (8 fl oz/250 ml) water

½ cup (4 oz/125 g) sugar

½ cup (4 fl oz/125 ml) soy sauce

Wash hijiki well in a large bowl of water. Any dust and sand will settle to bottom of bowl. Scoop hijiki from bowl and then soak in clean water for 20 minutes. Drain well. Place usuage in a bowl. Add boiling water to cover and soak for 3–4 minutes to remove some of oil. Remove from water, draining well. Cut usuage into strips ¼ inch (6 mm) wide. Heat oil in a saucepan over high heat. Add carrot strips and stir-fry until softened, about 2 minutes. Add hijiki and stir-fry for 2 minutes. Add usuage and stir-fry for 2 minutes. Add dashi and sugar, bring to a boil then reduce heat to medium-low and simmer for 4–5 minutes. Add soy sauce and cover pan with a slightly smaller lid. Cook for 20–30 minutes over medium-low heat, stirring occasionally. Liquid should reduce by two-thirds. Serve warm or cold.

Korean mung bean pancakes

Makes 15 pancakes

2 cups (14 oz/440 g) mung beans
water, for soaking
3 cups (24 fl oz/750 ml) extra water
⅓ cup (1½ oz/45 g) sticky rice powder
1½ oz (45 g) yellow (brown) onion
1 oz (30 g) Chinese cabbage kimchi
1 teaspoon table salt
5 daepa or scallions (shallots/spring onions),
   white parts only
2 oz (60 g) ground (minced) pork fillet
1 tablespoon finely chopped scallions
   (shallots/spring onions)
1 tablespoon crushed garlic
vegetable or sunflower oil, for frying

For dipping sauce
2 teaspoons light soy sauce
1 teaspoon white vinegar

Soak mung beans in water overnight to soften. Using your hands, rub soaked beans together to remove skins. Remove skins when they float to surface of water.

Transfer beans to a food processor and blend to a paste with extra water. Add sticky rice powder and mix with a spoon.

Finely slice onion and kimchi. Sprinkle with salt and lt stand for about 15 minutes to sweat (do not rinse off salt).

Cut white parts of 5 daepa or scallions into fine strips.

Mix pork with onion, kimchi, finely chopped scallion and garlic.

Add mung bean paste and mix to combine. Add salt to taste.

Heat 1 tablespoon oil in a wok. Ladle enough bean mixture into pan to make an 8-inch (20-cm) pancake. Cook until golden brown, about 3 minutes on each side.

To make dipping sauce: Combine soy sauce and white vinegar in a bowl.

Transfer pancakes to a plate and serve whole or sliced, accompanied by dipping sauce. Serve immediately. If pancake cools, reheat in heated wok for about 1 minute on each side.

Mango and yogurt curry

Serves 2

1 tablespoon vegetable oil

1 teaspoon brown mustard seeds

1 onion, cut into 8 wedges

1 teaspoon peeled and grated fresh ginger

1 large green Thai or Anaheim chili, seeded and sliced

¼ teaspoon chili flakes

1 teaspoon ground turmeric

12 curry leaves

1½ cups (12 oz/375 g) plain (natural) yogurt

3 mangoes, peeled, cut from pit, and sliced

sea salt to taste

1 tablespoon chopped fresh mint

In a large, heavy saucepan or wok, heat oil over medium heat and fry mustard seeds, onion, ginger, and chili for 2 minutes, or until onion is soft. Add chili flakes, turmeric, and curry leaves, and cook for 2 minutes. Remove from heat and stir in yogurt. Return to stove and cook over very low heat for 1 minute. Remove from heat, and add mangoes, salt, and mint. Stir until well combined. Serve warm immediately.

Mixed vegetable curry

Serves 4–6

1 tablespoon sticky (glutinous) rice
¼ cup (2 fl oz/60 ml) vegetable oil
¼ cup (2 fl oz/60 ml) red curry paste (see page 231)
1¼ cups (5 oz/150 g) chopped eggplant (aubergine)
¼ cup (1 oz/30 g) pea eggplants (optional)
4 long beans or 12 green beans, cut into
    1-inch (2.5-cm) pieces
½ cup (2 oz/60 g) canned or 1 cup (4 oz/125 g) fresh
    straw mushrooms, rinsed, drained and halved
½ cup (2 oz/60 g) coarsely chopped cauliflower florets
2 cups (16 fl oz/500 ml) vegetable stock (see page 221)
    or water
2 tablespoons soy sauce or fish sauce
4 fresh piper (beetle) leaves, or 2 cabbage leaves,
    coarsely chopped
7 fresh eryngo (sawtooth coriander) leaves or 6 sprigs
    cilantro (fresh coriander), coarsely chopped or torn
1 fresh long red chili, coarsely chopped
¼ teaspoon salt

In a wok or small frying pan over low heat, stir rice until
golden brown, 3–5 minutes. Transfer to a mortar and
pulverize with a pestle; set aside.

In a wok or large, heavy frying pan, heat oil over
medium–high heat and fry curry paste, stirring constantly,
until fragrant, 1–2 minutes. Add eggplants, beans,
mushrooms and cauliflower, and stir together well. Add
1 cup (8 fl oz/250 ml) stock or water, and simmer for
2 minutes. Add remaining stock or water and soy or fish
sauce. Bring to a boil.

Add remaining ingredients and ground rice. Bring to a boil,
then reduce heat and simmer for 2 minutes. Transfer to a
serving bowl and serve.

Tips

- If available, you can also add 1 cup dried cotton buds or
  kapok flowers (ngiu) at the same time as the eggplant,
  and/or 1 cup chopped acacia leaves at the end.
- You can add ¼ teaspoon prickly ash (kamchatton) with
  the chicken stock.

Mushroom and sesame stir-fry

Serves 4

2 tablespoons sesame oil

1 bunch scallions (shallots/spring onions), trimmed and
  sliced

8 oz (250 g) carrots, peeled and diced

1 red bell pepper (capsicum), seeded and sliced

1 green bell pepper (capsicum), seeded and sliced

1 yellow or orange bell pepper (capsicum), seeded
  and sliced

8 oz (250 g) button mushrooms, trimmed and halved
  or quartered

8 oz (250 g) zucchini (courgettes), trimmed and
  cut into sticks

1 tablespoon light soy sauce

1 tablespoon lemon juice

1 tablespoon clear honey

salt and pepper

1½ cups (6 oz/180 g) bean sprouts

1–2 tablespoons sesame seeds

In a wok or frying pan, heat oil and stir-fry scallions for
about 1 minute. Add carrots and bell peppers and cook
for 2–3 minutes, stirring frequently.

If mushrooms are tiny they may be left whole, otherwise
halve or quarter them then add to wok or pan with zucchini
and cook for a further 2–3 minutes.

Combine soy sauce, lemon juice and honey and add to
wok or pan. Season well with salt and pepper then add
bean sprouts. Cook for a further 2–3 minutes. Serve
generously sprinkled with sesame seeds.

Pumpkin dumplings in malai sauce

Serves 4–5

1 lb (500 g) pumpkin or butternut squash, peeled
and grated

2 large desiree or pontiac potatoes, 10 oz (300g) total,
boiled, peeled and mashed

¼ cup (⅓ oz/10 g) chopped cilantro (fresh coriander)

1 tablespoon finely grated fresh ginger

3 teaspoons finely chopped fresh green chilies

salt to taste

¼ cup (2 fl oz/60 ml) vegetable oil

1-inch (2.5-cm) cinnamon stick

4 green cardamom pods

4 whole cloves

1 small yellow (brown) onion, halved and thinly sliced

½ teaspoon salt, plus extra salt to taste

1 tablespoon finely grated fresh ginger

1 tablespoon crushed garlic

3 teaspoons ground turmeric

2 teaspoons chili powder

2 tomatoes, unpeeled, chopped

1 teaspoon honey

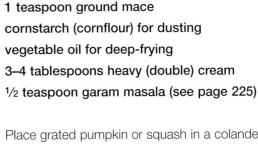

1 teaspoon ground mace

cornstarch (cornflour) for dusting

vegetable oil for deep-frying

3–4 tablespoons heavy (double) cream

½ teaspoon garam masala (see page 225)

Place grated pumpkin or squash in a colander and squeeze well to extract any excess water. Place in a bowl with potatoes, cilantro, ginger and chilies. Season with salt and mix well. Set aside.

To make sauce: In a wok, heat oil over medium–low heat. Add cinnamon, cardamom and cloves, and cook until fragrant, about 30 seconds. Add onion and ½ teaspoon salt, and cook uncovered, stirring often, until onion is dark golden brown, 10–15 minutes. Stir in ginger and garlic, and cook for 30 seconds. Add turmeric and chili powder, and cook, stirring, for 30 seconds. Stir in tomatoes and cook, stirring, until tomatoes soften, 3–4 minutes. Stir in honey and mace. Cover to keep warm.

Meanwhile, shape pumpkin mixture into walnut-sized balls, dust with cornstarch and place on a baking sheet dusted with cornstarch. Fill a medium saucepan with oil to a depth of 3 inches (7.5 cm). Heat oil over medium–high heat to 375°F (190°C) on a deep-frying thermometer. Carefully add dumplings in batches of five and cook until golden brown, 2–3 minutes. Remove with a slotted spoon and drain on paper towels.

Place dumplings on a serving dish. Stir cream into sauce and pour over dumplings. Sprinkle with garam masala, season with extra salt to taste, and serve hot.

Tip

Dumplings are best shaped and cooked close to serving time. The mixture can be made 2 hours ahead and kept at room temperature.

Stir-fried Asian greens with tempeh

Serves 4

canola oil for deep-frying

3 garlic cloves, thinly sliced

8 dried shiitake mushrooms

3 tablespoons soybean oil

5 oz (150 g) tempeh, cut into thin strips

8 oz (250 g) firm tofu, drained and diced

1 medium yellow (brown) onion, cut into thin wedges

1 clove garlic, finely chopped

8 water chestnuts, thinly sliced, or 6 slices lotus root

14 ears fresh baby corn, halved lengthwise

3 small bunches baby bok choy, chopped

1 cup (2 oz/60 g) soybean sprouts, tails trimmed

⅓ cup (3 oz/90 g) ketjap manis with
    1 tablespoon light soy

1 small red chili, seeded and finely chopped

fried shallots (French shallots), for garnish, optional

steamed jasmine rice, for serving

Fill a small wok or saucepan one-third full of oil and heat to 350°F (180°C). Cook garlic slices until golden, about 1 minute. Drain on paper towels.

Soak mushrooms in warm water until soft, about 20 minutes. Squeeze out excess water, discard stems and thinly slice tops. In a wok or frying pan, heat 2 tablespoons oil over medium-high heat and stir-fry tempeh and tofu slices until lightly browned, 3–4 minutes. Remove and drain on paper towels. Add remaining oil to pan and stir-fry onion and garlic until onion is soft. Add tempeh, tofu, water chestnuts, baby corn, bok choy and soybean sprouts and stir-fry until bok choy is wilted, about 3 minutes. Stir in ketjap manis and chili and cook for 2 more minutes to blend flavors. Garnish with garlic flakes and shallots and serve with steamed jasmine rice.

Stir-fried choy sum with ginger

Serves 4

3 tablespoons fish sauce

3 tablespoons water

2 teaspoons peeled and grated fresh ginger

2 tablespoons vegetable oil

1 bunch choy sum, about 16 oz (500 g), trimmed
    and cut into 3-inch (7.5-cm) lengths

In a small bowl, combine fish sauce, water and ginger.
Warm vegetable oil in a wok over medium heat. Add choy
sum and stir-fry until slightly softened and color intensifies,
about 3 minutes. Stir in fish sauce mixture and toss until
choy sum is well coated. Cover and cook for 2 minutes.
Serve hot.

Stir-fried fennel, celery, snow peas and bean sprouts

Serves 4

2 cloves garlic, roughly chopped

½ cup (½ oz/15 g) cilantro (fresh coriander) leaves

1 stalk lemongrass, bottom 3 inches (7.5 cm) only, inner stalks roughly chopped

juice of 1 lime

2 tablespoons soy sauce

2 tablespoons superfine (caster) sugar

sea salt and freshly ground black pepper to taste

2 tablespoons vegetable oil

1-inch (2.5-cm) piece fresh ginger, peeled and finely chopped

1 green chili, seeded and thinly sliced

12 scallions (shallots/spring onions), roots trimmed, sliced

2 bulbs fennel, roots and leaves trimmed and thinly sliced

2 celery stalks, sliced

3½ oz (105 g) snow peas (mange-tout)

⅔ cup (5 fl oz/150 ml) thick coconut cream

3½ oz (105 g) bean sprouts, rinsed

¼ cup (1½ oz/45 g) unsalted roasted peanuts

steamed jasmine rice, for serving

Place garlic, cilantro, lemongrass and lime juice in a mortar and using a pestle, pound into a smooth paste. Alternatively, place in a small food processor and process to form a smooth paste, about 20 seconds. Transfer to a bowl and add soy sauce, sugar, and salt and pepper to taste.

In a wok or large frying pan, heat oil over medium heat. Add ginger, chili and scallions, and stir-fry until aromatic, about 2 minutes. Add fennel, celery and snow peas, and stir-fry for 3 minutes. Add spice paste and coconut cream and cook, continuing to stir, until sauce thickens slightly, about 2 minutes. Stir in bean sprouts. Remove from heat.

Sprinkle with peanuts and serve immediately with steamed jasmine rice.

Stir-fried vegetables

Serves 4

1 tablespoon vegetable oil

1 small carrot, cut into matchstick strips

½ yellow (brown) onion, thinly sliced

¼ green bell pepper (capsicum), thinly sliced

10 snow peas (mange-tout), halved if large

6 leaves Chinese napa cabbage, shredded

1 cup (4 oz/125 g) bean shoots

1 teaspoon salt

1 teaspoon sugar

1 teaspoon instant dashi

1 tablespoon mirin

Preheat a wok or large frying pan over high heat until very hot, then add oil. Add carrot and onion and stir-fry until softened, about 2 minutes. Add bell pepper and snow peas, then cabbage and bean shoots. Stir-fry until carrot and onion are soft and snow peas and cabbage are wilted. Add salt, sugar, dashi and mirin. Continue to stir-fry until flavors are blended and vegetables are cooked to your liking, about 3 minutes. Serve hot.

Stir-fried vegetables with soy and ginger

Serves 4

1 yellow (brown) onion, cut into thin wedges

3 baby white bok choy, washed and coarsely
   chopped

3 baby green (shaughai) bok choy, washed and
   coarsely chopped

1 medium fresh jkama (yam bean), peeled and thinly
   sliced, or 1 can (7 oz/220 g) water chestnuts,
   drained

2 tablespoons Japanese soy sauce

1 teaspoon grated fresh ginger

1 cup (2 oz/60 g) fresh soybean sprouts,
   tails trimmed

In a large wok, combine all ingredients, cover and cook
over medium-low heat until vegetables are just tender but
still crisp, 3–4 minutes, tossing occasionally. Do not
overcook. Serve immediately.

Tip

Substitute other Asian greens such as Chinese broccoli
(gai lan), Chinese flowering cabbage (choy sum) and/or tat
soi for the bok choy. Also, substitute soy sauce with rinsed
fermented black soybeans.

Stuffed eggplants

Serves 4–8

8 medium-sized Japanese (long) eggplants (aubergines)
3 medium-sized yellow (brown) onions
6 tablespoons olive oil
4 cloves garlic, chopped
3 medium tomatoes, peeled and chopped
3 tablespoons chopped fresh flat-leaf (Italian) parsley
salt
freshly ground black pepper
2 tablespoons lemon juice
pinch sugar
½ cup (4 fl oz/125 ml) water

Remove stems from eggplants or leave intact if desired. At intervals along length of each eggplant, peel off strips of skin, ½ inch (12 mm) wide, to create a striped effect. Cut a deep lengthwise slit on one side of each eggplant, without cutting all the way through eggplant, stopping short of ends.

Slice each onion lengthwise, then cut into slender wedges. In a large wok or frying pan over medium–low heat, heat 3 tablespoons oil. Add onion and fry until translucent, about 8 minutes. Add garlic and cook for 1 minute. Place onions and garlic in a bowl and combine with chopped tomatoes, parsley and salt and pepper to taste.

Heat remaining 3 tablespoons oil in same wok over high heat. Add eggplants and fry until lightly browned on all sides but still rather firm, about 10 minutes. Remove wok or pan from heat and turn eggplants slit-side up.

Spoon vegetable mixture into slits, forcing in as much filling as possible. Spread remaining filling on top. Add lemon juice, sugar and water to wok or pan and cover tightly. Cook over low heat until eggplants are tender, about 45 minutes. Add more water only if liquid in pan evaporates.

Let cool to room temperature and serve as an appetizer or a light meal with bread, or as an accompaniment.

Sweet-and-sour potatoes

Serves 4

1 lb (500 g) uniformly sized desiree or pontiac
    potatoes, (about 3–4 medium)

salt as needed

3 tablespoons vegetable oil

½ teaspoon brown or black mustard seeds

36 fresh curry leaves

½ teaspoon ground turmeric

½ cup (4 fl oz/125 ml) coconut milk

¼ cup (⅓ oz/10 g) chopped cilantro (fresh coriander)

4 teaspoons finely chopped fresh green chilies

1 teaspoon sugar

juice of 1 lemon

Place potatoes and large pinch salt in a saucepan with
enough cold water to cover. Bring to a boil over
medium–high heat. Reduce heat to medium–low and cook,
partially covered, until potatoes are tender, about 20
minutes. Drain potatoes and let cool for 15 minutes. Peel
potatoes and cut into 1½-inch (4-cm) cubes. Set aside.

In a wok, heat oil over medium–low heat. Add mustard
seeds and cook until they crackle, about 30 seconds.
Add curry leaves and turmeric, and cook, stirring, for
15 seconds. Add potatoes and season with salt. Toss
gently to combine. Add coconut milk, cilantro, chilies
and sugar, and simmer, gently stirring occasionally, for
2 minutes. Drizzle with lemon juice and serve hot.

Tofu and vegetable stir-fry

Serves 4

⅓ cup (3 fl oz/90 ml) vegetable oil

6½ oz (200 g) firm tofu, cut into 1-in (2.5-cm) cubes

3 cloves garlic, crushed

2 teaspoons peeled and grated fresh ginger

2 onions, cut into eighths

1 bunch Chinese broccoli, trimmed and cut into
   1½-in (4-cm) lengths

3½ oz (105 g) snow peas (mange-tout), trimmed
   and sliced crosswise

1 red bell pepper (capsicum), seeded and sliced

1 cup (6 oz/180 g) drained canned baby corn

1 bunch bok choy, trimmed and cut into 1½-in
   (4-cm) lengths, or 1 bunch spinach, trimmed

2 tablespoons oyster sauce

1 tablespoon light soy sauce

steamed white rice, for serving

In a wok over medium heat, warm vegetable oil. Working in batches, add tofu and stir-fry until golden on all sides, 2–3 minutes. Using slotted spoon, remove from wok and drain on paper towels. Pour off all but 2 tablespoons oil from wok and return to medium heat. Add garlic, ginger and onions and stir-fry until softened, 2–3 minutes. Add broccoli, snow peas, bell pepper, corn and bok choy or spinach. Stir-fry until vegetables are tender-crisp, 3–4 minutes. Add tofu and oyster and soy sauces and gently stir-fry until heated through, 1–2 minutes.

Serve hot, accompanied with steamed white rice.

Vegetarian green curry

Serves 4

5 oz (150 g) firm tofu, drained then cut
    into ¾-inch (2-cm) cubes
1 cup (8 fl oz/250 ml) vegetable oil
2 cups (16 fl oz/500 ml) coconut milk
1–2 tablespoons vegetable oil (optional)
¼ cup (2 fl oz/60 ml) fresh or commercial green
    curry paste (page 231)
½ cup (2 oz/60 g) chopped eggplant (aubergine)
    or 3 round Thai eggplants, chopped
½ cup (2 oz/60 g) pea eggplants (optional)
1 cup (4 oz/125 g) coarsely chopped fresh or canned
    bamboo shoots, rinsed and drained
6 ears fresh or canned baby corn, rinsed and drained,
    cut into bite-sized pieces
2 tablespoons palm sugar
2 kaffir lime leaves, stemmed
1 cup (1 oz/30 g) loosely packed fresh sweet Thai
    basil leaves
2 tablespoons soy sauce
1 fresh long green chili, cut into large pieces, for
    garnish
1 fresh long red chili, cut into large pieces, for garnish

Pat tofu dry with a paper towel. In a large wok, heat oil and, working in batches, fry tofu cubes until golden. Remove using a slotted spoon and drain on paper towels; reserve.

Let coconut milk stand, allowing the thick coconut milk to rise to the top. Spoon thick coconut milk into a small bowl, reserving 2 tablespoons for garnish.

In a wok or large, heavy frying pan, heat thick coconut milk over medium-high heat for 3–5 minutes, stirring constantly, until it separates. If it does not separate, add optional oil. Add green curry paste and fry, stirring constantly, until fragrant, 1–2 minutes. Add vegetables and fried tofu and

stir until well coated. Add remaining thin coconut milk and bring to a boil. Reduce heat and simmer until vegetables are slightly soft, about 4 minutes.

Add palm sugar—if using a wok, add it along the edge of the wok so that it melts before stirring into the curry; if using a standard frying pan, add directly to the curry. Tear kaffir lime leaves and basil into pieces. Stir in soy sauce, kaffir lime leaves and half the basil.

Remove from heat and transfer to a serving bowl. Drizzle over reserved 2 tablespoons thick coconut milk. Garnish with green and red chilies, and remaining basil leaves and serve.

Vegetarian stir-fry

Serves 4

2 tablespoons sesame or walnut oil

1 large onion, peeled and thinly sliced

4 celery stalks, thinly sliced

8 oz (250 g) carrots, peeled and cut into strips

2–4 oz (50–100 g) pecan or walnut halves

1 red bell pepper (capsicum), seeded and cut into
   strips

8–12 oz (250–375 g) zucchini (courgettes), trimmed and
   thinly sliced

1–1½ lb (500–750 g) white cabbage, finely shredded

4 oz (125 g) pitted dates, halved

salt and pepper

1 tablespoon lemon juice

freshly chopped parsley

In a wok, heat oil and fry onion briskly until beginning to color. Add celery and carrots and continue cooking for 3–4 minutes, stirring occasionally.

Stir in pecans or walnuts, bell pepper and zucchini and stir-fry, for 3–4 minutes. Add cabbage and dates and continue to stir-fry for 3–4 minutes.

Season well with salt and pepper and add lemon juice. Stir to heat through thoroughly and serve in a warmed dish liberally sprinkled with parsley.

rice and noodles

Bell peppers and mushrooms with noodles

Serves 4

5 oz (150 g) fresh egg noodles

6 Chinese dried mushrooms

1 tablespoon vegetable oil

1 teaspoon Asian sesame oil

1 red bell pepper (capsicum), seeded and sliced

1 yellow bell pepper (capsicum), seeded and sliced

1 cup (4 oz/125 g) fresh bean sprouts, rinsed

4 oz (125 g) fresh shiitake mushrooms, sliced

4 oz (125 g) fresh oyster mushrooms, sliced if large

¼ cup (2 fl oz/60 ml) sweet chili sauce

1 tablespoon light soy sauce

¼ cup (¼ oz/7 g) cilantro (fresh coriander) leaves, for garnish

Bring saucepan of water to a boil. Add noodles and cook until tender, about 3 minutes. Drain and set aside.

Place dried mushrooms in small bowl, add boiling water to cover and allow to stand until softened, 10–15 minutes. Drain and squeeze out excess liquid. Thinly slice mushrooms, discarding thick stems.

In a wok, heat vegetable and sesame oils over medium heat. Add bell peppers, bean sprouts and fresh mushrooms and stir-fry until slightly softened, 1–2 minutes. Add noodles, reconstituted mushrooms and chili and soy sauces and stir-fry until heated through, 2–3 minutes.

Serve hot, garnished with cilantro leaves.

Chili broccoli with noodles

Serves 4

12 oz (375 g) egg noodles
1½ lb (750 g) broccoli, cut into florets
3 tablespoons olive oil
1 medium red (Spanish) onion, chopped
2 cloves garlic, crushed
1 small red chili pepper, seeded and thinly sliced
sea salt and freshly ground black pepper to taste
balsamic vinegar, for drizzling
⅓ cup (1½ oz/45 g) parmesan shavings, for serving

Cook noodles as directed on package or on page 29, then drain and rinse. Meanwhile, bring a saucepan of water to a boil. Add broccoli florets and cook for 2 minutes. Drain and refresh in cold water. Drain again and set aside.

In a wok or large frying pan, heat oil. Add onion, garlic and chili pepper and stir-fry until onion softens, about 2 minutes. Stir in broccoli and cooked noodles. Stir-fry until heated through, about 3 minutes. Season with salt and pepper to taste.

Serve hot, drizzled with balsamic vinegar and topped with parmesan shavings.

Chili fried rice

Serves 4

3 tablespoons vegetable oil

1 onion, chopped

1 small red chili, seeded and chopped

1 tablespoon red curry paste (see page 231)

5 oz (150 g) pork fillet, thinly sliced

12 jumbo shrimp (king prawns), peeled and deveined, tails intact

4 cups (20 oz/625 g) cooked white rice, chilled

2 eggs, beaten

1 tablespoon fish sauce

½ cup (1½ oz/45 g) chopped scallions (shallots/spring onions)

⅓ cup (½ oz/15 g) chopped cilantro (fresh coriander)

3 small red chili flowers (see page 25) (optional)

In a wok, heat oil over medium–high heat. Add onion and chili and stir-fry until onion is softened, about 2 minutes. Stir in curry paste and cook for 1 minute. Add pork and stir-fry until pork changes color, 3–4 minutes. Add shrimp and stir-fry until shrimp change color, about 3 minutes. Add rice and stir-fry until rice is coated with oil.

Push rice to one side of wok. Add beaten eggs and allow to partially set without stirring, then mix with rice. Stir in fish sauce, scallions and cilantro.

Serve hot as main course or as accompaniment to stir-fried dishes. Garnish with chili flowers, if desired.

Chinese fried rice

Serves 4

2 eggs

pinch of salt

4 scallions (spring onions/shallots) with some
   green tops

½ red or green bell pepper (capsicum)

½ stick celery

4 oz (125 g) roasted or barbecued pork, chicken,
   or leg ham

3 tablespoon peanut or vegetable oil

7 oz (220 g) can shrimp (prawns), drained

3 cups cooked white or brown rice

½ cup (2 oz/60 g) cooked green peas

2 tablespoon chicken stock (see page 220)

1½ tablespoon Chinese rice wine or dry sherry

2 teaspoon soy sauce

Whisk together eggs and salt until blended. Cut scallions, bell pepper, celery and meat into thin slivers.

In a wok or large, heavy-based frying pan, heat 1 tablespoon oil over medium heat. Add eggs and cook stirring, until scrambled but not dry. Remove from pan and set aside.

Heat remaining oil in pan until hot. Add scallions, vegetables, meat and shrimp and stir-fry 45–60 seconds.

Add rice to pan and stir-fry until rice is heated through, 2–3 minutes. Stir in reserved egg and peas.

Stir together sauce ingredients and drizzle over rice. Toss lightly to mix well. Serve immediately.

Fried cellophane noodles

Serves 4–6

6 oz (180 g) cellophane (bean thread) noodles

¼ cup (2 fl oz/60 ml) vegetable oil

3 eggs, beaten

1 onion, cut into wedges

3 firm tomatoes, cut into 4 or 8 wedges

3 cloves pickled garlic, coarsely chopped

2 tablespoons fish sauce

3 tablespoons oyster sauce

1 teaspoon granulated (white) sugar

½ teaspoon ground white pepper

2 scallions (shallots/spring onions), finely chopped

Soak noodles in cold water for at least 15 minutes, to soften. Drain and coarsely cut with scissors into 6-inch (15-cm) lengths.

In a wok or large, heavy frying pan, heat half oil (2 tablespoons) over medium–high heat. Add eggs and stir-fry until cooked and dry, 1–2 minutes. Remove with a slotted spoon and reserve. Add remaining 2 tablespoons oil to wok. Add noodles and stir-fry while adding onion, tomatoes and pickled garlic. Stir-fry for 1 minute to heat through, then add fish sauce, oyster sauce, sugar and pepper and stir until well combined. Add three-quarters scallions and eggs, stir to combine and remove from heat. Transfer to a serving dish, sprinkle with remaining scallion and serve.

Fried glass noodles with fish or eel

Serves 4

1 lb (500 g) skinless fish or eel fillets
  (see Tip below), finely diced

2 tablespoons fish sauce

½ teaspoon ground pepper

12 dried black mushrooms

leaves from 2 large sprigs Vietnamese mint or
  spearmint

1 bunch Chinese (flat/garlic) chives

6½-oz (200-g) packet cellophane (bean thread) noodles

about 1 cup (8 fl oz/250 ml) vegetable oil, for frying

2 onions, thinly sliced

6 cloves garlic, crushed

2 cups (4 oz/125 g) bean sprouts, rinsed and drained

2 fresh long red chilies, seeded and cut into thin strips

2 lemons, cut into wedges

Asian chili sauce, for serving (optional)

In a medium bowl, combine fish or eel, fish sauce and pepper. Stir well and refrigerate until ready to use, at least 20 minutes.

Soak mushrooms in hot water for 20 minutes, then drain, squeezing to remove all liquid. Use scissors or a small knife to cut tough stems; discard. Cut mushroom caps into small dice and set aside.

Stack a few Vietnamese mint leaves together and roll tightly into a cylinder. Use a sharp knife to cut crosswise into thin shreds. Repeat with remaining leaves. Cut chives into 1½-inch (4-cm) pieces.

Prepare noodles as described on page 29. Using scissors, cut noodles in manageable lengths for serving.

Transfer fish to a plate, reserving marinade in bowl, and pat fish dry with paper towels. In a wok or large frying pan, heat oil over medium–high heat until it shimmers. Add one-third of fish and stir-fry until almost crisp, 3–5 minutes. Transfer to paper towels to drain.

Reduce heat to medium, draining all but ¼ cup (2 fl oz/ 60 ml) of the oil. Add remaining fish plus marinade and mushrooms, and stir-fry for 3 minutes. Then add noodles and stir-fry for 2 minutes. Finally, add chives, onion, garlic, bean sprouts, reserved fried fish and remaining marinade. Stir-fry for 1 minute and sprinkle with Vietnamese mint. Transfer to a serving plate, and garnish with the reserved crispy-fried fish and chilies. Serve with lemon wedges, and chili sauce if desired.

Tip

This is a very old Hanoi recipe, and popular restaurants there specialize in eel dishes. Sturgeon is probably the closest in texture to eel, although tender catfish fillets, as well as oily garfish and smelt, can also be substituted.

Fried noodles with pork

Serves 4

8 oz (250 g) fresh or dried egg noodles

1 tablespoon vegetable oil

1 bunch Chinese broccoli, cut into 3-in (7.5-cm) lengths

8 oz (250 g) Chinese barbecue pork, sliced

½ cup (5 oz/150 g) chunky peanut butter

2 teaspoon Asian sesame oil

2 tablespoons light soy sauce

2 teaspoons garam masala (see page 225)

3 cloves garlic, crushed

1 small red chili, seeded and chopped

Bring saucepan of water to boil. Add noodles and cook until tender, about 3 minutes for fresh noodles, about 5 minutes for dried noodles. (If using precooked noodles, soak in boiling water for 8–10 minutes.) Drain and keep warm.

In a wok, heat vegetable oil over medium–high heat. Add broccoli and pork and stir-fry for 4 minutes. In small bowl, combine peanut butter, sesame oil, soy sauce, garam masala, garlic and chili. Mix until well combined. Add peanut butter mixture and noodles to wok. Raise heat to high and stir-fry until heated through, about 1 minute. Do not overcook.

Serve hot.

Fried rice with pineapple

Serves 4–6

¼ cup (2 fl oz/60 ml) vegetable oil

2 Chinese sausages, cut in small rounds

2 tablespoons butter

½ teaspoon curry powder

3 cups (15 oz/470 g) cooked long-grain jasmine rice

1 small onion, coarsely chopped

3 scallions (shallots/spring onions), chopped

1 firm tomato, coarsely chopped

½ cup (3 oz/90 g) raisins (sultanas)

½ cup (3 oz/90 g) coarsely chopped fresh pineapple
    pieces, or canned in water, and drained

1 teaspoon granulated (white) sugar

2 tablespoons soy sauce

In a wok or large, heavy frying pan, heat oil over medium–high heat and fry sausages for 1 minute. Using a slotted spoon, transfer to paper towels to drain.

Add butter and curry powder to wok and stir-fry, stirring constantly, until fragrant, about 1 minute. Stir in cooked rice until well coated. Add sausages, onion, scallions, tomato, raisins and pineapple. Stir-fry for about 4 minutes, then add sugar and soy sauce.

Tip

For an impressive presentation, place a pineapple on its side on a cutting board and slice in half or slice off the top third lengthwise. Scoop flesh from bottom half or two-thirds to make a cavity. Set aside ½ cup (3 oz/90 g) pineapple for recipe, and save rest for another use. Spoon fried rice into hollowed-out pineapple, cover with "lid," and serve.

Garlic and cumin lentils

Serves 4

1 cup (7 oz/220 g) masoor dhal (dried red lentils)
⅔ cup (5 fl oz/150 ml) chicken stock (see page 220)
   or water
½ teaspoon peeled and finely chopped fresh ginger
½ teaspoon ground coriander
1 tablespoon ghee or vegetable oil
2 teaspoons toasted cumin seeds
1 medium onion (5 oz/150 g), sliced
2 cloves garlic, crushed
1 fresh long green chili, seeded and thinly sliced
   (optional)
1 tablespoon finely chopped fresh mint

Place lentils in a sieve and wash under cold running water. Pick over, and remove any foreign matter. Soak in water for a minimum of 1 hour. Drain well and place in a dish that will fit a bamboo steamer or steamer basket. Add stock, ginger and coriander, stir well, and place bowl in steamer.

Partially fill a wok or pot with water (steamer should not touch water) and bring to a rapid simmer. Place steamer over water, cover, and steam until lentils are soft, about 30 minutes.

In a medium pan, heat ghee and cook cumin seeds, onion, garlic and chili until onion browns, 8–10 minutes, stirring occasionally. Stir mint and half of onion mixture into lentils. Spread remaining onion mixture on top for garnish. Serve as a dip or side dish with crispy fried pappadums.

Tip

Lentils can be cooked for less time to retain shape (if not being mashed), and used in salads or as a vegetable.

Ginger-coconut rice

Serves 4

2 tablespoons vegetable oil

1 teaspoon chili oil

1 onion, chopped

1 red bell pepper (capsicum), seeded and chopped

3 cloves garlic, crushed

3 teaspoons peeled and grated fresh ginger

1½ cups (10½ oz/330 g) short-grain white rice

1½ cups (12 fl oz/375 ml) chicken stock (see page 220)

1 cup (8 fl oz/250 ml) water

½ cup (4 fl oz/125 ml) coconut milk

3 scallions (shallots/spring onions)

3 tablespoons chopped cilantro (fresh coriander)

2 tablespoons unsweetened shredded coconut, toasted

3 tablespoons lemon juice

¼ cup (1 oz/30 g) unsweetened shredded coconut,
   for serving

In a wok, heat vegetable and chili oils over medium–high heat. Add onion, bell pepper, garlic and ginger and stir-fry until softened, about 3 minutes. Add rice and stir until well coated with oil, about 2 minutes.

Add stock, water and coconut milk and bring to a boil. Reduce heat to low, cover and simmer until all liquid is absorbed and rice is tender, 15–20 minutes. Remove from heat and stir in scallions, cilantro, toasted coconut and lemon juice.

Serve hot, topped with shredded coconut.

Herb and lemon noodle salad with ponzu dressing

Serves 4

For dressing

¼ cup (2 fl oz/60 ml) fresh lemon juice

1 tablespoon soybean oil

1 tablespoon soy sauce

2 teaspoons grated lemon zest (rind)

2 scallions (shallots/spring onions), green parts, finely sliced

1 medium red chili, seeded and finely chopped (optional)

1 tablespoon soybean oil

4 oz (125 g) firm tofu, cut into strips ¾ x 1 inch (2 x 2.5 cm)

1 cup (2 oz/60 g) soybean sprouts

4 oz (125 g) dried soba noodles

1 cup (2 oz/60 g) shredded spinach leaves

1 cup (1½ oz/40 g) finely chopped mixed fresh herbs such as parsley, chives, oregano, basil

1 cup (6 oz/185 g) finely chopped celery

1 English (hothouse) cucumber, seeded and finely diced, unpeeled

To make dressing: In a small bowl, combine all dressing ingredients and whisk until blended. Set aside.

In a large wok, heat oil over medium heat and stir-fry tofu until golden, about 2 minutes each side. Cook soybean sprouts in boiling water for 2 minutes. Using a skimmer, remove sprouts. Rinse under cold water, then drain. Return water to a boil, gradually add noodles and return to a boil. Add ¼ cup (2 fl oz/60 ml) cold water and bring back to a boil. Add another ¼ cup cold water, return to a boil and cook noodles until tender, 8–10 minutes total cooking time. Drain noodles, add remaining ingredients and dressing, toss well to combine, and serve.

Indian noodle stir-fry

Serves 2–4

2 tablespoons peanut oil

1 onion, chopped

1 tomato, chopped

2 tablespoons chives or scallions (shallots/spring
onions), chopped

2 teaspoons curry paste

1–2 tablespoons tomato ketchup (sauce)

1 tablespoon chili sauce or minced chili, or to taste

2 teaspoons soy sauce, preferably light

1 lb (500 g) hokkein egg noodles

2–4 tablespoons cooked stock (see page 220) or water

2 eggs, lightly beaten (optional)

In wok or large frying pan, heat oil. Add onion and fry over
medium heat until soft. Add tomato and chives and cook
for a few minutes. Add curry paste, sauces and stock and
simmer gently for a few minutes. Add noodles and toss
through to heat. Pour over beaten egg and leave to set for
about 45 seconds on hot noodles. Mix through and serve.

Tips

- Yellow hokkein noodles can be bought fresh in sealed
  plastic bags from the refrigerated section of
  supermarkets, delicatessens, and Chinese food stores.
  They'll keep refrigerated for over a week, even longer if
  frozen.
- Add whatever takes your fancy. Some suggestions are:
  blanched Chinese long (snake) beans cut into pieces,
  squares of tofu, 4 oz (125 g) raw peeled shrimp
  (prawns), cubes of boiled potato, green peas, bean
  sprouts, shredded lettuce or cabbage, sliced zucchini
  (courgette) and mushrooms, and strips of green pepper
  (capsicum). Raw vegetables or meat should be sautéed
  after, or with, the onion.

Indian pilaf

Serves 4

1¼ cups (9 oz/280 g) basmati rice
1 tablespoon vegetable oil
1 onion, chopped
2 cloves garlic, finely chopped
1 teaspoon fennel seeds
1 tablespoon sesame seeds
½ teaspoon ground turmeric
1 teaspoon ground cumin
½ teaspoon sea salt
2 whole cloves
3 cardamom pods, lightly crushed
6 black peppercorns
1¾ cups (14 fl oz/440 ml) chicken stock (see page 220)
fresh curry leaves, for garnish

Rinse rice in several changes of cold water until water runs clear. Put rice in a bowl and add cold water to cover. Let stand for 30 minutes. Drain.

In a medium, heavy saucepan, heat oil over medium heat and fry onion and garlic until onion is soft, 1–2 minutes. Stir in fennel, sesame seeds, turmeric, cumin, salt, cloves, cardamom pods, and peppercorns. Fry until fragrant, 1–2 minutes. Add drained rice, and fry, stirring constantly, for 2 minutes, or until rice is opaque. Pour in stock and bring to a boil. Cover, reduce heat to low, and simmer until rice is tender and all liquid has been absorbed, 15–20 minutes. Remove from heat and let stand, covered, for 5 minutes. Spoon into serving bowls and garnish with curry leaves.

Metropole fried rice

Serves 6

For omelet
4–6 eggs
4 tablespoons water
pinch sugar
pinch salt (optional)
vegetable oil, for cooking

vegetable oil, for cooking
2 large onions, coarsely chopped
4 oz (125 g) shelled shrimp (prawns), coarsely chopped
1½ cups (9 oz/280 g) diced cooked chicken meat,
   firmly packed
½ cup (4 fl oz/125 ml) fish sauce or to taste
¼ green bell pepper (capsicum), seeded and
   finely diced
¼ red bell pepper (capsicum), seeded and finely diced
4 cups (18 oz/ 550g) cold steamed rice
2 teaspoons ground pepper
1 tablespoon Asian chili sauce or more to taste
cilantro (fresh coriander) sprigs, for garnish
shrimp crackers, for serving (optional)

To make a single omelet: Using a fork, beat egg(s)—you
can use one egg or two to make a single omelet—until
blended. Add 1 tablespoon water and sugar, and salt if
using. Heat an 8-inch (20-cm) frying pan over medium heat.
Add enough oil to coat bottom. It should sizzle if hit with a
drop of water. Pour beaten egg into pan, lifting pan to tilt it
quickly to allow egg to spread out evenly. Reduce heat to
low and cook just until set, about 30 seconds. Carefully flip
over omelet and cook a few seconds on second side. It
shoud be firm and not runny. Transfer to a plate to cool,
then roll, cut into strips and set aside. Prepare 4 omelets
this way.

In a large frying pan or wok, heat 2 tablespoons oil over
high heat and stir-fry onions until barely wilted, about
1 minute. Add shrimp and chicken, and stir-fry for 2 minutes.
Season with half of fish sauce, add bell peppers, and stir-fry
for 1 minute. Add rice, pepper, chili sauce and remaining
fish sauce to taste. Reduce heat to medium–high and stir-
fry for 5 minutes.

Moisten six individual rice bowls or small ramekins and
pack with fried rice. Alternatively, press all rice into a lightly
oiled 6-cup (48-fl oz/ 1.5-L) bowl. Press firmly, then unmold
into center of a plate. Sprinkle with omelet strips and
cilantro. If desired, accompany with shrimp crackers.

Mushroom and noodle stir fry

Serves 4

6 Chinese dried mushrooms

6½ oz (200 g) rice stick noodles, wheat flour noodles
   or egg noodles

1 tablespoon vegetable oil

3 cloves garlic, crushed

8 oz (250 g) fresh shiitake mushrooms, brushed clean
   and sliced

8 oz (250 g) fresh oyster mushrooms, brushed clean
   and sliced

1 cup (3 oz/90 g) chopped scallions (shallots/spring
   onions)

3 tablespoons rice wine

2 tablespoons soy sauce

⅓ cup (½ oz/15 g) cilantro (fresh coriander) leaves

Place dried mushrooms in small bowl, add boiling water to cover and let stand for 10 minutes. Drain and squeeze out excess liquid. Slice mushrooms, discarding tough stems.

Cook noodles as directed on package or on page 29. Drain and set aside.

In wok or frying pan, heat oil over medium–high heat. Add garlic, fresh mushrooms and scallions and stir-fry until slightly softened, about 3 minutes. Stir in rice wine, soy sauce and noodles. Cook until heated through, about 2 minutes. Remove from heat and stir in cilantro. Serve immediately.

Nasi goreng

Serves 4–6

3 teaspoons peeled and grated fresh ginger

1 teaspoon ground turmeric

1 teaspoon shrimp paste

2 teaspoons chili sauce

3 tablespoons peanut oil

1 onion, chopped

3 cloves garlic, crushed

½ red bell pepper (capsicum), seeded and chopped

1 celery stalk, chopped

1 carrot, peeled and chopped

½ cup (2½ oz/75 g) thawed frozen peas

4 oz (125 g) Chinese barbecue pork, chopped

1 cup (4 oz/125 g) fresh bean sprouts, rinsed

1 cup (3 oz/90 g) shredded bok choy

4 cups (20 oz/625 g) cold cooked jasmine rice

4 oz (125 g) cooked shrimp (prawns), peeled and
deveined, tails intact

¼ cup (2 fl oz/60 ml) coconut milk

2 tablespoons light soy sauce

In a small bowl, combine ginger, turmeric, shrimp paste and
chili sauce. Mix to form paste. Set aside.

In wok, heat peanut oil over medium–high heat. Add onion
and garlic and stir-fry until onion softens, about 1 minute.
Stir in spice paste, bell pepper, celery, carrot, peas, pork,
bean sprouts and bok choy. Raise heat to high and stir-fry
until vegetables soften slightly, 3–4 minutes. Add rice
and shrimp and stir-fry until rice is heated through, about
3 minutes. Combine coconut milk and soy sauce, add to
wok and stir until evenly combined and mixture is hot.

Spoon into individual bowls. Serve hot as a main course or
as an accompaniment to other stir-fried dishes.

Noodles with baked vegetables

Serves 4

8 oz (250 g) fresh or dried egg noodles or udon noodles

1 lb (500 g) butternut squash (pumpkin), cut into
   1-inch (2.5-cm) pieces

2 carrots, peeled and cut into 1-inch (2.5-cm) pieces

3 tablespoons vegetable oil

5 cloves garlic, crushed

6½ oz (200 g) zucchini (courgettes), cut into
   1-inch (2.5-cm) pieces

2 onions, chopped

1 cup (8 fl oz/250 ml) coconut milk

¼ cup (⅓ oz/10 g) chopped cilantro (fresh coriander)

1 small red chili, seeded and chopped

salt and ground pepper to taste

Preheat oven to 400°F (200°C/Gas 6). Bring saucepan of water to boil. Add noodles and cook until tender, about 2½ minutes for fresh udon noodles, about 3 minutes for fresh egg noodles, about 5 minutes for dried egg noodles, 10–12 minutes for dried udon noodles. Drain and set aside.

In baking dish, combine squash, carrots, 2 tablespoons vegetable oil and 3 cloves garlic. Toss to coat vegetables in oil. Bake, uncovered, for 15 minutes. Remove from oven, add zucchini, stir vegetables, return to oven and bake until vegetables are tender, about 15 minutes longer.

In wok over medium–high heat, warm remaining 1 tablespoon vegetable oil. Add onions and remaining 2 cloves garlic and stir-fry until onions soften, 2–3 minutes. Add coconut milk, cilantro and chili. Stir until heated through, 3–4 minutes. Add baked vegetables and noodles. Cook until heated through, 1–2 minutes. Taste and season with salt and pepper.

Divide among individual bowls and serve immediately.

Noodles with squash and green papaya

Serves 4

250 g (8 oz) rice stick noodles

2 tablespoons vegetable oil

2 cloves garlic, crushed

1 lb (500 g) butternut squash (pumpkin), peeled
and cut into 1-inch (2.5-cm) cubes

13 oz (400 g) green papaya, grated

¾ cup (6 fl oz/180 ml) chicken stock (see page 220)

2 eggs, beaten

2 tablespoons fish sauce

Cook noodles as directed on package or on page 29. Drain and set aside. In wok or frying pan, heat oil over medium–high heat. Add garlic and squash and cook until garlic is golden, about 2 minutes. Add papaya and stock. Reduce heat to low and simmer, covered, until squash is tender and stock is absorbed, about 15 minutes.

Push squash mixture to one side of wok or pan and raise heat to medium. Add eggs and cook, without stirring, until partially set. Stir gently until eggs are scrambled. Stir eggs into squash mixture. Stir in noodles and fish sauce. Cook until heated through, about 1 minute.

Divide among individual plates and serve immediately.

Pad Thai noodles

Serves 4–6

6 oz (180 g) dried rice noodles

3 tablespoons vegetable oil

3 oz (90 g) firm tofu, rinsed and patted dry, cut
   into small cubes

2 large cloves garlic, finely chopped

1 tablespoon dried shrimp

⅓ cup (3 fl oz/90 ml) chicken stock (see page 220)
   or water

3 tablespoons fish sauce

1 tablespoon soy sauce

1–2 tablespoons tamarind purée, to taste

2–3 tablespoons granulated (white) sugar, to taste

2 eggs, beaten

3 tablespoons chopped roasted peanuts

1 small bunch Chinese (garlic or flat) chives, or regular
   chives, cut into 1-inch (2.5-cm) pieces

1 cup (2 oz/60 g) bean sprouts

2 limes, cut into wedges

Soak noodles in cold water for about 10 minutes to soften;
drain and set aside.

In a wok or large, heavy frying pan, heat oil over high heat.
Add tofu, garlic and dried shrimp and stir-fry until garlic
begins to brown, about 1 minute. Add noodles and stir-fry
carefully, so as not to break them. Add stock or water and
continue cooking until noodles are tender, 2–3 minutes.
Reduce heat to medium and add fish sauce, soy sauce,
tamarind and sugar. Cook until mixture sputters, then add
eggs, and stir-fry constantly until eggs are cooked and dry,
about 1–2 minutes. Add peanuts, chives and bean sprouts,
and stir to mix.

Transfer to a serving dish and serve, garnished with lime
wedges.

Tips

- Pad Thai is a popular Thai dish found in all parts of the
  kingdom. The noodles used here are about the thickness
  of a bean sprout. You can substitute 14 oz (400 g) fresh
  rice noodles, but do not pre-soak.
- For a striking presentation, fry a thin, flat omelet in a
  nonstick pan (see page 187), and fold this over the fried
  noodle mixture. Make a small incision at the top to
  expose the contents, and serve.

Salmon laksa

Serves 4

6½ oz (200 g) cellophane (bean thread) noodles

3 small red chilies, seeded and chopped

3 cloves garlic

1 piece peeled fresh ginger, about 2½ in (6 cm) long

½ cup (2/3 oz/20 g) cilantro (fresh coriander) leaves

3 teaspoons vegetable oil

1 teaspoon Asian sesame oil

4 cups (32 fl oz/1 L) coconut milk

3 cups (24 fl oz/750 ml) fish stock (see page 221)

8 oz (250 g) salmon fillet, skin and errant bones
   removed, sliced into 12 thin slices

2 tablespoons lemon juice

1 tablespoon fish sauce

4 scallions (shallots/spring onions), sliced, for garnish

¼ cup (¼ oz/7 g) fresh mint leaves, for garnish

Place noodles in bowl and soak in boiling water for 10 minutes. Drain and set aside.

Place chilies, garlic, ginger and cilantro in food processor. Process to form smooth paste.

In a wok, heat vegetable and sesame oils over medium–high heat. Add spice paste and cook until aromatic, about 1 minute. Add coconut milk and stock and bring to a boil. Reduce heat to low and simmer, uncovered, for 10 minutes. Add salmon, lemon juice and fish sauce and simmer until salmon is opaque, 2–3 minutes.

To serve, divide noodles among individual bowls. Ladle soup over noodles. Sprinkle each serving with scallions and mint leaves.

Soba noodles with bell peppers

Serves 4

6½ oz (200 g) soba noodles
1 tablespoon vegetable oil
2 teaspoons Asian sesame oil
3 cloves garlic, crushed
2 teaspoons peeled and grated fresh ginger
½ teaspoon red pepper flakes
1 onion, chopped
1 red bell pepper (capsicum), seeded and sliced
1 yellow bell pepper (capsicum), seeded and sliced
2 small zucchini (courgettes), julienned
5 oz (150 g) green beans, trimmed
3 tablespoons soy sauce
2 tablespoons rice wine

3 teaspoons palm sugar or brown sugar
1½ tablespoons Worcestershire sauce
⅓ cup (1½ oz/45 g) unsalted roasted peanuts, chopped

In a wok or frying pan, heat vegetable and sesame oils over medium–high heat. Add garlic, ginger, red pepper flakes and onion and cook until aromatic, about 1 minute. Add bell peppers, zucchini and beans and stir-fry until slightly softened, about 3 minutes. Combine soy sauce, rice wine, sugar, Worcestershire sauce and noodles. Add to wok or pan and stir-fry until heated through, about 2 minutes.

To serve, divide among individual plates and top with peanuts. Serve immediately.

Spicy cellophane noodle salad

Serves 4–6

4 oz (125 g) cellophane (bean thread) noodles

2 cups (16 fl oz/500 ml) coconut milk or water

4 oz (125 g) ground (minced) pork

12 jumbo shrimp (king prawns), shelled and deveined

2–3 tablespoons fish sauce, to taste

2 tablespoons fresh lime juice

5 cloves pickled garlic

1 tablespoon thinly sliced shallots (French shallots),
   preferably pink

10–20 fresh small red chilies, thinly sliced, to taste

½ cup (2 oz/60 g) coarsely chopped celery, preferably
   Chinese celery

1 firm tomato, halved and thinly sliced

1 oz (30 g) fresh or dried cloud or tree ear mushrooms
   (black or white fungus), trimmed and rinsed, soaked
   if dried (optional)

½ cup (¾ oz/20 g) coarsely chopped cilantro (fresh
   coriander)

Soak noodles in cold water for 10 minutes to soften. (If
required, noodles can be prepared several hours in
advance, left in the water until ready to use.) Drain and
coarsely cut with scissors into 6-inch (15-cm) lengths.

In a wok or large saucepan over high heat, bring 1 cup
(8 fl oz/250 ml) coconut milk or water to a boil. Add pork,
stirring vigorously to break meat apart, and cook for
2 minutes. Drain, reserving ¼ cup (2 fl oz/60 ml) of the
liquid. Set meat aside. In the same wok or saucepan, bring
remaining coconut milk or water to a boil over high heat.
Add shrimp and cook, stirring constantly, until evenly pink,
about 1 minute. Drain and set shrimp aside. (If desired,
reserve this cooking liquid for another dish. Do not use it to
flavor salad.)

In a large pot bring water to a boil, then pour boiling
water into a heatproof bowl. Plunge noodles in and soak
for 1 minute; drain, then soak in cold water for 1 minute.
(Be precise with these timings, as you do not want the
noodles to become water-logged.)

In a large bowl, combine reserved cooking liquid, fish
sauce, and lime juice. Add garlic, shallots, chilies to taste,
celery, tomato, and mushrooms if using. Toss together, then
add noodles. Transfer to a serving plate, sprinkle cooked
pork and shrimp over, garnish with cilantro, and serve
immediately.

Tips

- Purchase individual small packets of cellophane noodles,
  or a packet of small bunches, as they are difficult to pry
  apart in large bunches.

- For a less spicy salad, simply bruise the whole chilies;
  do not cut them.

Steamed rice in lotus parcels

Serves 6

4 cups (18 oz/540 g) cold steamed rice

25 dried black mushrooms

¼ cup (1½ oz/45 g) dried lotus seeds (optional)

3 tablespoons vegetable oil

2 cups (10 oz/300 g) diced cooked chicken meat,
   firmly packed

2 teaspoons salt

1 teaspoon ground pepper

2–3 scallions (shallots/spring onions), including
   green parts, coarsely chopped

2 tablespoons fish sauce

1–2 large fresh or dried lotus leaves
   (see Tips below)

Soak mushrooms in hot water for 20 minutes, then drain, squeezing to remove all liquid. Use scissors or a small knife to cut tough stems; discard. Cut mushroom caps into small dice and set aside. If using dried lotus seed, soak in warm water for 20 minutes, then use a toothpick inserted from end to end to remove any bitter green sprouts. Cook lotus seed in gently boiling water until tender, about 20 minutes; drain and set aside.

In a wok, heat 2 tablespoons of the oil over medium–high heat. Add mushroom, chicken and lotus seed, if using, and stir-fry for 5 minutes. Season with salt and pepper and transfer to bowl.

In same wok, heat remaining 1 tablespoon of oil over medium–high heat and stir-fry rice and scallions for 5 minutes. Season with fish sauce. Add chicken and mushrooms and mix well.

If using a dried lotus leaf, cover it with boiling water to soften, then drain. The water will become brown and somewhat murky. Fresh leaves should be wiped to remove any grit or sediment.

Spread out leaf and pile steamed rice mixture in middle. Press lightly to compact the pile into a 10-x-7-inch (25-x-18-cm) mound, 2–3 inches (5–7 cm) high. Leave a 5-inch (13-cm) clearance on all sides. Fold the two sides over each other as if folding an envelope, leaving narrow ends still exposed. Fold one end over, then hold packet upright. Lightly press to compress rice, then fold remaining end over to enclose firmly. Tie packet securely both crosswise and lengthwise with coarse kitchen string. The dish can be prepared to this point up to 1 hour ahead, or 3–4 hours if refrigerated.

Place parcel in a steamer over rapidly boiling water. Cover and steam until heated throughout, about 5 minutes. (Refrigerated parcels will require 15–20 minutes of steaming.) Carefully remove from steamer. To serve, use scissors to cut open parcel, rolling back lotus for a decorative appearance.

Tips

- Large, voluptuous lotus leaves are imbued with a slight taste of chestnut. Fresh lotus is available from May to September in Southeast Asia, but dried leaves are more commonly sold overseas. If unavailable, don't enclose the rice mixture in a parcel but serve hot, directly from wok or pan.
- For individual servings, use 6 lotus leaves and divide filling equally into 6 portions. Place 1 portion onto each leaf. Fold as above.

desserts

Almond cream pudding

Serves 6

3 tablespoons ground rice
3 cups (24 fl oz/750 ml) milk
pinch of salt
¼ cup (2 oz/60 g) sugar
¾ cup (3 oz/90 g) ground blanched almonds
1 tablespoon rosewater
chopped pistachios or almonds, for garnish
pomegranate seeds (optional)

In a small bowl, mix ground rice in ¼ cup (2 fl oz/60 ml) milk. In a large wok, bring remaining milk to a boil. Stir in ground rice mixture, salt and sugar.

Reduce heat to medium and cook, stirring constantly with a wooden spoon, until mixture bubbles gently. Reduce heat to low and simmer for 5 minutes, stirring often so mixture cooks slowly and does not scorch.

Stir in ground almonds until blended smoothly, then add rosewater. Remove from heat and stir occasionally until mixture cools slightly.

Pour into a serving bowl or six individual small bowls.

Chill in refrigerator and serve garnished with chopped nuts, and with pomegranate seeds if desired.

Banana tempura

Serves 4

1 egg
1 cup (8 fl oz/250 ml) ice cold water
1⅓ cups (7 oz/220 g) tempura flour
vegetable oil, for deep-frying
4 bananas, sliced in half lengthwise
½ cup (2½ oz/75 g) all-purpose (plain) flour
2 tablespoons superfine (caster) sugar
4 scoops vanilla ice cream

In a bowl, beat egg lightly. Add water and continue to beat lightly. Mix in tempura flour; do not overmix. Batter should be slightly lumpy.

Pour oil in a deep, heavy-bottomed wok or pan to fill 3 inches (7.5 cm) deep. Heat oil until it reaches 375°F (190°C) on a deep-frying thermometer. Working in batches, dredge banana pieces in flour, shaking off excess, then dip in batter, allowing excess to drain away. Carefully slip bananas into hot oil. When batter is beginning to set, use chopsticks to drip a little extra batter on bananas. Cook until bananas are light golden brown, 3–4 minutes. Using a wire skimmer, remove bananas from oil and drain on paper towels. Arrange 2 pieces banana on each serving plate. Sprinkle lightly with sugar and serve with a scoop of ice cream.

Chinese lemon, date and walnut cake

Makes 9-inch (23-cm) square cake

4 eggs

⅔ cup (5 oz/150 g) white sugar

2 teaspoons grated lemon zest (rind)

1 cup (5 oz/150 g) all-purpose (plain) flour, sifted

2 tablespoons coarsely chopped walnuts

2 tablespoons coarsely chopped dates

½ teaspoon ground cinnamon

Put eggs in a bowl and beat until frothy, about 2 minutes. Add half of sugar and beat until light and fluffy, 2–3 minutes. Add remaining sugar and lemon zest and beat for 10 minutes.

Gradually stir flour into egg mixture. Do not add too quickly, or flour will sink to bottom. Grease a 9-inch (23-cm) square cake pan, and spoon in half mixture. Sprinkle with half of nuts and dates and carefully spoon in remaining egg mixture. Sprinkle top with remaining nuts and dates, then cinnamon. Cover pan loosely, to allow for rising, with a double layer of greased plastic wrap or parchment (baking) paper, or place a kitchen towel under steamer lid to keep any condensation from falling on cake. Place in a large steamer and cover.

Partially fill a wok or pot with water (steamer should not touch water) and bring to a rapid simmer. Place over water, cover, and steam until a skewer inserted in cake comes out clean, about 15 minutes. Cut cake into squares or slices and serve warm or cold with fresh fruit or fruit coulis and fresh cream.

Cream and berry stack

Serves 4

vegetable oil, for deep-frying
8 wonton wrappers
8 oz (250 g) ricotta cheese
½ cup (4 fl oz/125 ml) heavy (double) cream
4 tablespoons confectioners' (icing) sugar, sifted
2 teaspoons Grand Marnier
1 teaspoon grated orange zest (rind)
5 oz (155 g) fresh raspberries
5 oz (155 g) fresh strawberries, hulled (stemmed)
   and sliced
3 oz (90 g) fresh blueberries

In a wok or frying pan, heat oil until it reaches 375°F (190°C) on a deep-frying thermometer or until a small bread cube dropped in oil sizzles and turns golden. Working in batches, add wonton wrappers and fry until golden on both sides, about 1 minute. Using slotted spoon, remove from pan and drain on paper towels. Allow to cool.

In bowl, combine ricotta cheese, cream, 3 tablespoons of sugar, Grand Marnier and zest. Using electric mixer beat until light and fluffy, 2–3 minutes. Cover and chill until ready to serve.

In another bowl, combine raspberries, strawberries and blueberries. Cover and chill.

To serve, place one wonton on each plate. Spread with ricotta filling. Spoon berries over filling. Top with second wonton. Dust with some of the remaining sugar.

Creamy coconut black rice

Serves 4–5

1 cup (7 oz/220 g) black glutinous rice

1 cup (8 fl oz/250 ml) cold water

1½ cups (12 fl oz/375 ml) thin coconut cream or
   coconut milk

⅓ cup palm or brown sugar

2 teaspoons grated lime or lemon zest (rind)

pinch salt

1 cup (8 fl oz/250 ml) thick coconut cream (optional)

1 medium (12 oz/375 g) mango, peeled and sliced, for
   serving

Place rice in a bowl and add cold water to cover. Let soak overnight, drain, and rinse well under cold running water. Place rice and water in a bowl that fits in a bamboo steamer or steamer basket.

Partially fill a wok or pot with water (steamer should not touch water) and bring to a rapid simmer. Place steamer over water, cover, and steam until rice is tender, 40–45 minutes, stirring occasionally. Remove from heat and stir in thin coconut cream, sugar, lime zest, and salt. Cover and steam until thickened to consistency of hot cereal, 15–20 minutes. Swirl thick coconut cream through, if desired, and serve with sliced mango. Alternatively, cut a small cantaloupe (rockmelon) in half, scoop out seeds, and fill with rice.

Figs in syrup

Serves 6–8

1 lb (500 g) dried figs
4 cups (32 fl oz/1 L) cold water
⅓ cup (2 oz/60 g) whole blanched almonds
¾ cup (6 oz/185 g) granulated sugar
thin strip lemon zest (rind)
juice of 1 lemon
3 tablespoons honey
chopped almonds, pistachios or walnuts, for garnish
whipped cream or plain (natural) yogurt, for garnish

Rinse figs well, place in a bowl and add cold water. Let stand for 8 hours until plump. Drain off water into a large wok.

Insert an almond into each fig from bottom. Set aside.

Add sugar to water in the wok and cook over medium heat, stirring occasionally, until sugar dissolves. Add lemon zest, juice and honey, and bring to a boil. Add stuffed figs and return to a boil. Reduce heat to low and cook, uncovered, until figs are tender and syrup is thick, about 30 minutes. Remove lemon zest and discard.

Arrange figs upright in a bowl. Pour syrup over figs, let cool, cover, and chill in refrigerator.

Sprinkle with chopped nuts and serve with whipped cream or yogurt.

Ginger and nutmeg sweet potato pudding

Makes 6

10 oz (300 g) sweet potato (kumara), peeled and
  roughly chopped
1 cup (8 fl oz/250 ml) thick coconut cream
¼ cup (2 oz/60 g) brown sugar
2 eggs, beaten
2 teaspoons peeled and grated fresh ginger
2 teaspoons freshly grated nutmeg or 2 teaspoons
  ground nutmeg
whipped cream, for garnish (optional)

Preheat oven to 350°F (180°C/Gas 4). Line a bamboo steamer with parchment (baking) paper or use a heatproof plate. Half fill a wok with water (steamer should not touch water) and bring water to a boil. Arrange sweet potato in steamer, cover and place steamer in wok. Cook sweet potato until tender, adding more water to wok when necessary, about 15 minutes. Lift steamer from wok, carefully remove sweet potato from steamer and transfer to a bowl. Mash with a fork or potato masher until smooth. Set aside and allow to cool.

Place sweet potato, coconut cream, brown sugar, eggs, ginger and nutmeg in a food processor and process until smooth. Pour into 6 Chinese teacups or other heatproof molds. Place on a baking sheet (tray) and cook until firm to the touch, about 20 minutes. Remove from oven. Serve warm or chilled, garnished with whipped cream if desired.

Hot mocha and brandied raisin soufflé

Makes 6 small soufflés or 1 large

For brandy-soaked raisins
⅓ cup (2 oz/60 g) raisins (sultanas)
1 cup (8 fl oz/250 ml) brandy

4 oz (125 g) dark chocolate
¼ cup (2 oz/60 g) superfine (caster) sugar
4 eggs, separated, plus 1 extra egg white
1 teaspoon instant coffee granules
⅓ cup (3 fl oz/90 ml) brandy-soaked raisins

Place raisins in an airtight jar and cover with brandy. Cover jar and soak overnight. Drain to use.

Lightly butter six 1-cup (8-fl oz/250-ml) ramekins or a 6-cup (48-fl oz/1.5-L) soufflé dish. Put chocolate in a bowl and place bowl in a bamboo steamer or steamer basket. Place uncovered, over wok or pot of simmering water, to melt chocolate. Remove from heat and add sugar, stirring until dissolved. Lightly beat 4 egg yolks and coffee and stir into chocolate, mixing gently. In a large bowl, beat 5 egg whites until stiff, glossy peaks form. Stir one-third of egg whites into chocolate mixture, then lightly fold in remaining whites. Drain raisins and divide them among prepared ramekins. Spoon chocolate mixture onto raisins. Cover each ramekin with a piece of buttered parchment (baking) paper or buttered plastic wrap.

Partially fill a 12-inch (30-cm) wok or pot with water (steamer should not touch water) and bring to a rapid simmer. Arrange ramekins on both levels of a two-level steamer, or large soufflé dish on one level. Place over water, cover, and steam until set, 12–15 minutes (switch levels halfway through for even cooking), although soufflé will still be slightly sticky inside. Serve immediately, or refrigerate and serve chilled.

Grand Marnier crème caramels

Serves 6

⅓ cup (3 oz/90 g) white sugar
3 tablespoons water
4 eggs
2 tablespoons superfine (caster) sugar
2½ cups (20 fl oz/625 ml) milk
1 teaspoon vanilla extract (essence)
1 tablespoon Grand Marnier
1 teaspoon grated orange zest (rind)

In a small saucepan, combine white sugar and 3 tablespoons water and melt sugar over low heat, stirring constantly. Increase heat and boil until mixture caramelizes to a golden brown color, 4–5 minutes. Be careful not to let it burn. Immediately pour into six 1-cup (8- fl oz/250-ml) ramekins, while tipping each ramekin to cover sides with caramel.

Beat eggs and superfine sugar together until well combined. Stir in milk, vanilla, Grand Marnier and zest. Pour custard into ramekins and cover with oiled aluminum foil or a double layer of plastic wrap.

Partially fill a 12-inch (30-cm) wok or pot with water (steamer should not touch water) and bring to a rapid simmer. Put ramekins in 2 stacked bamboo steamers or 2-level steamer basket. Place steamer over water, cover, and steam until custard has set, about 20 minutes (an inserted skewer will come out clean when custard is cooked). Switch baskets halfway through for even cooking. Remove from steamer and cool to room temperature. Cover each ramekin with a fresh sheet of plastic wrap, and refrigerate until required.

To serve, place a plate over each custard and invert. Serve with fresh berries.

Lime and coconut pudding with lime-ginger syrup

Serves 6

¾ cup (6 oz/180 g) butter

⅓ cup (3 oz/90 g) superfine (caster) sugar

1 teaspoon grated lime zest (rind)

1 teaspoon vanilla extract (essence)

3 eggs

1 cup (5 oz/150 g) self-rising flour, sifted

1 cup (4 oz/125 g) unsweetened dried shredded
   (desiccated) coconut

½ cup (4 oz/125 g) decorating (crystal) sugar

3 tablespoons lime juice

1 tablespoon shredded lime zest (rind)

1 tablespoon peeled and shredded fresh ginger

whipped cream, for serving

Butter six ½-cup (4-fl oz/125-ml) ramekins and line bottoms with parchment (baking) paper. Set aside.

In a bowl, combine butter, sugar and lime zest. Using electric mixer, beat until light and creamy, 3–4 minutes. Add vanilla. Add eggs, one at a time, beating well after each addition. If mixture begins to curdle, add 1 tablespoon all-purpose (plain) flour. Fold in flour and coconut and mix well.

Spoon pudding into prepared ramekins. Cover each with piece of buttered parchment paper. Half fill wok with water (steamer should not touch water) and bring water to a boil. Arrange ramekins in steamer, cover and place steamer over boiling water. Steam until puddings are firm to touch, 40–45 minutes. Add more water to wok when necessary.

In a small saucepan over low heat, combine sugar, lime juice and zest, and ginger. Stir until sugar dissolves. Bring to a boil and let boil for 2 minutes. Remove from heat.

Slowly pour warm syrup over warm puddings. Serve garnished with whipped cream.

Panfried pineapple

Serves 4

¾ cup (6 oz/180 g) unsalted butter
1 small pineapple (about 1½ lb/750 g), peeled, cut
 lengthwise into quarters, cored and thinly sliced
¾ cup (6 oz/180 g) packed brown sugar
¼ cup (2 fl oz/60 ml) dark rum or brandy

Melt butter in large frying pan over medium heat. Add pineapple slices and cook for 1 minute. Sprinkle evenly with brown sugar and cook, turning pineapple occasionally, until sugar is melted and pineapple is translucent, 2–3 minutes. Add rum or brandy, stir to combine and cook 1 minute.

To serve, place pineapple on plates and spoon warm sauce over top.

Polenta pudding with mango sauce

Makes 6

½ cup (4 oz/125 g) butter

⅔ cup (5 oz/150 g) white sugar

2 teaspoons grated lemon zest (rind)

2 eggs

1 cup (5 oz/150 g) self-rising flour

½ teaspoon baking powder

¼ teaspoon salt

⅔ cup (3½ oz/100 g) polenta

½ cup (4 fl oz/125 ml) sour cream

⅓ cup (3 fl oz/90 ml) milk

2 mangoes, peeled, pitted and sliced

2 tablespoons confectioners' (icing) sugar

2 tablespoons lime juice

1 teaspoon grated lime zest (rind)

Butter six ½-cup (4-fl oz/125-ml) ramekins and line bottoms with parchment (baking) paper. Set aside.

In a bowl, combine butter, sugar and lemon zest. Using electric mixer, beat until light and creamy, 3–4 minutes. Add eggs, one at a time, beating well after each addition. If mixture begins to curdle, add 1 tablespoon all-purpose (plain) flour.

Sift flour, baking powder and salt into bowl. Stir in polenta. Combine sour cream and milk. Fold flour mixture into egg mixture alternately with sour cream mixture. Mix well.

Spoon pudding into prepared ramekins. Cover each with piece of buttered parchment paper. Half fill wok with water (steamer should not touch water) and bring water to a boil. Arrange ramekins in steamer, cover and place steamer over boiling water. Steam until puddings are firm to touch, 45–50 minutes. Add more water to wok when necessary.

In a food processor, combine mangoes, sugar and lime juice and zest. Process until smooth.

Remove steamer from wok and carefully remove ramekins from steamer. Run sharp knife around sides of each ramekin. Invert onto plate and unmold pudding. Serve warm with mango sauce.

Rose water doughnuts

Makes 30 doughnuts

For yogurt sauce
¾ cup (6 fl oz/180 g) plain (natural) yogurt
3 teaspoons rose water
1 tablespoon confectioners' (icing) sugar, sifted

2¼ cups (11 oz/330 g) self-rising flour, sifted
½ cup (2 oz/60 g) ground almonds
⅓ cup (3 oz/90 g) butter or ghee, plus 2 cups
   (16 fl oz/500 ml) vegetable oil or ghee, for
   deep-frying
⅓ cup (3 fl oz/90 ml) plain (natural) yogurt
¼ cup (2 fl oz/60 ml) warm water
2 teaspoons rose water
grated zest (rind) of 1 orange
⅓ cup (2½ oz/75 g) superfine (caster) sugar

In a small bowl, combine yogurt, rose water and sugar. Mix well. Cover and refrigerate until ready to serve.

In a bowl, combine flour and almonds. Using fingertips, rub ⅓ cup (3 oz/90 g) butter or ghee into flour. Stir in yogurt, warm water, rose water and orange zest. Mix to form soft dough. Turn out onto floured work surface. Knead until smooth, about 2 minutes. Divide dough into 30 pieces. Roll each into ball.

In a wok, heat 2 cups (16 fl oz/500 ml) vegetable oil or ghee until it reaches 375°F (190°C) on a deep-frying thermometer or until a small bread cube dropped into oil sizzles and turns golden. Working in batches, add doughnuts and deep-fry until golden, 5–6 minutes. Using slotted spoon, remove from wok and drain on paper towels. Place sugar on plate and roll each doughnut in sugar until well coated. Serve warm with yogurt sauce.

Spicy fruit salad

Serves 4

1¼ cups (10 fl oz/300 ml) water

½ cup (4 oz/125 g) decorating (crystal) sugar

juice and zest (rind) of 1 orange

3 star anise

6 whole black peppercorns

6 whole cardamom pods

3 cinnamon sticks

3 peaches, peeled, pitted and sliced

4 fresh figs, quartered

1½ cups (6½ oz/200 g) blueberries

2 oranges, peeled and cut into segments

In a wok, combine water, sugar, orange zest and juice, star anise, peppercorns, cardamom and cinnamon. Place over low heat and stir until sugar dissolves.

Raise heat to medium and bring to a boil. Reduce heat to low and simmer, uncovered, for 10 minutes. Remove from heat.

Add peaches, figs, blueberries and oranges. Allow to cool to room temperature and serve warm or refrigerate for 30 minutes and serve chilled.

Sweet date wontons

Makes 24 wontons

6½ oz (200 g) dates, pitted and chopped

½ cup (2 oz/60 g) walnuts, chopped

6½ oz (200 g) fresh or canned lychees, pitted and chopped

1 tablespoon grated orange zest (rind)

24 wonton wrappers

1 egg, beaten

vegetable oil, for deep-frying

2 tablespoons confectioners' (icing) sugar, sifted

In a bowl, combine dates, walnuts, lychees and orange zest. Mix well. Place wonton wrappers on work surface and cover with damp kitchen towel. Working with one wrapper at a time, lay on work surface and place 1 teaspoon filling in center. Brush edges of wonton with egg, gather edges and twist to seal. Repeat with remaining wonton wrappers.

In a wok or frying pan, heat oil until it reaches 375°F (190°C) on a deep-frying thermometer or until a small bread cube dropped in oil sizzles and turns golden. Working in batches if necessary, add wontons and fry until golden, 1–2 minutes. Using slotted spoon, remove from wok or pan and drain on paper towels. Let cool.

Sprinkle with confectioners' sugar and serve.

sauces, stocks and condiments

Adjat sauce

Makes about ¾ cup (6 fl oz/180 ml)

⅓ cup (3 oz/90 g) granulated (white) sugar

⅓ cup (3 fl oz/90 ml) water

2 tablespoons rice vinegar

¼ cup (2 oz/60 g) peeled, thinly sliced cucumber

1½ tablespoons ground roasted peanuts

1 tablespoon thinly sliced shallots (French shallots),
    preferably pink

1 tablespoon coarsely chopped cilantro (fresh
    coriander) leaves and stems

¼ fresh long red chili, coarsely chopped

In a small saucepan over low heat, combine sugar and water and stir until sugar dissolves. Increase heat, bring syrup to a full boil, and cook without stirring for a few minutes. Remove from heat and let cool. Stir remaining ingredients into syrup and serve.

Tips

This sauce traditionally accompanies both massaman and yellow curries, although it is rarely served in restaurants today. It may also be served with meat satay, but if doing so, omit the peanuts.

Chili jam

Makes about 1¾ cups (14 fl oz/440 ml)

2 whole bulbs garlic
4 oz (125 g) shallots (French shallots), preferably pink
15 dried long red chilies
1 cup (8 fl oz/250 ml) vegetable oil
2 tablespoons palm sugar
1 tablespoon granulated (white) sugar
¼ teaspoon salt

Preheat oven to 400°F (200°C/Gas 6). Lightly break the unpeeled garlic bulb by pressing down on a knife handle with the heel of your hand, so that the cloves sit loosely together, but do not separate cloves from bulb completely. Separately wrap garlic and shallots in aluminum foil. Roast on top shelf of oven until soft to touch, about 30 minutes. Remove from oven and let cool in foil. Peel shallots and garlic.

Roast chilies by tossing them in a wok or large, heavy frying pan over high heat until lightly brown, 2–3 minutes. Remove stems, but retain the seeds. In a large mortar, grind chilies to a powder with a pestle. Add roasted garlic and shallots and pound until smooth. (Or, place chilies in a food processor to grind, then add garlic and shallots and process until smooth.)

Store in a covered jar for up to 6 months in the refrigerator. Do not drain off any oil from the top, as this helps to preserve the jam.

Tip
Chili jam is served in Thailand as a table condiment, much like ketchup and mustard in the West.

Sweet chili relish

Makes about 5 cups (40 fl oz/1.25 L)

2 cups (8 oz/250 g) peeled and finely
    shredded daikon
2 jars pickled garlic, 1lb (500 g) each, drained
    and chopped
1½ cups (12 fl oz/375 ml) rice vinegar
¾ cup (1 oz/30 g) chopped cilantro (fresh coriander)
    roots and stems
7 fresh long red chilies, finely chopped
3½ cups (28 oz/875 g) granulated (white) sugar
¼ teaspoon salt

In a wok or large saucepan, combine all ingredients and slowly bring to a boil. Reduce heat, then simmer for 20 minutes. Remove from heat and let cool completely. Store in a tightly covered jar in the refrigerator for up to 1 month.

Tips
- To save time, prepare ingredients that require chopping in a food processor.
- This sauce originates from Thailand and it is fast becoming a standard table condiment in the West. Traditionally, it accompanies Thai fish cakes, grilled or fried dishes, and squid rings and spring rolls.

Pictured opposite
Front: Adjat sauce
Center: Chili jam
Back: Sweet chili relish

Chicken stock

Makes 8 cups (64 fl oz/2 L)

1 chicken, whole, about 2 lb (1 kg)
1 large onion, roughly sliced
1 large carrot, peeled and chopped
2 celery stalks, chopped
5 cilantro (coriander) stems, including roots
1 teaspoon sea salt
8 black peppercorns
10 cups (80 fl oz/2.5 L) water

Place chicken, onion, carrot, celery, cilantro, salt and peppercorns in a large saucepan and cover with water.

Place over medium–high heat and bring liquid to a boil.

Reduce heat to medium–low and simmer for 1–1½ hours, skimming surface occasionally to remove scum and fat.

Remove saucepan from heat. Remove chicken and strain liquid. Allow stock to cool completely, then remove remaining fat from surface.

Tips

- To enhance the Asian flavor of this stock, add 5 or 6 slices fresh ginger or galangal, or a 2-inch (5-cm) piece of lime zest (rind), or 2 fresh (or 4 dried) kaffir lime leaves.
- Stock can be refrigerated for 5 days, or frozen for up to 3 months.
- Chicken meat may be pulled from bones and reserved for another use.
- To make beef stock, substitute chicken with beef cuts and bones.

Fish stock

Makes 8 cups (64 fl oz/2 L)

about 2 lb (1 kg) heads and bones of 2 medium-sized
   white-fleshed fish
2 tablespoons light olive oil
1 large onion, roughly chopped
1 large carrot, peeled and roughly chopped
2 celery stalks, with leaves, roughly chopped
3 stems fresh flat-leaf (Italian) parsley
3 stems cilantro (fresh coriander), preferably including
   roots
3 fresh or 6 dried kaffir lime leaves (optional)
8 black peppercorns
1 teaspoon sea salt

Wash fish heads and bones well, removing any gills. Chop
bones so that they fit into a large pot.

In a large pot, heat oil over high heat for 1 minute. Add fish
heads and bones and cook, stirring and turning heads and
bones, until any remaining flesh starts to cook and is slightly
golden, 4–5 minutes.

Add remaining ingredients and stir to combine. Add
enough water to cover bones completely (approximately
8 cups/64 fl oz/2 L) and bring liquid to a steady simmer.
Reduce heat to medium and simmer for 25 minutes. Skim
any scum from surface as stock simmers.

Strain liquid through a very fine sieve. If you don't have a
very fine sieve, line your sieve with a double layer of damp
cheesecloth (muslin). Discard solids.

Let cool then cover with plastic wrap and refrigerate if not
using immediately.

Tip

Fish stock can be refrigerated for 2 days. If stored in tightly
covered containers, it can be frozen for 2 months.

Vegetable stock

Makes 6 cups (48 fl oz/1.5 L)

2 tablespoons oil
4 large yellow brown onions, unpeeled and chopped
2 large parsnips, unpeeled and chopped
2 large carrots, unpeeled and chopped
5 sticks celery, including leaves, chopped
2 bay leaves
fresh bouquet garni
1 teaspoon whole black peppercorns
12 cups (96 fl oz/3 L) water

Preheat oven to 400°F (200°C/Gas 6). In a large baking
dish, heat the oil. Add the chopped onion, carrot and
parsnip and toss to coat in oil. Bake for 30 minutes, until
lightly golden.

Transfer vegetables to a large heavy-based pan. Add
remaining ingredients and bring to boil slowly. Reduce heat
and simmer, uncovered, for 1 hour, until reduced by half.

Strain liquid through a very fine sieve. Discard solids. Let
cool then cover with plastic wrap and refrigerate if not using
immediately.

Tip

Vegetable stock can be refrigerated for 5 days, or frozen for
up to 3 months.

Chili and coriander dipping sauce

Makes 2 cups (16 fl oz/500 ml)

4 cloves garlic, chopped
1 lemongrass stalk, chopped, or 2 teaspoons
   grated lemon zest (rind)
1 tablespoon chili paste
2 tablespoons fish sauce
1 cup (8 fl oz/250 ml) lemon juice
1 cup (8 fl oz/250 ml) rice wine vinegar
⅓ cup (2 oz/60 g) superfine (caster) sugar
1 teaspoon cornstarch (cornflour) mixed with
   1 tablespoon water
½ cup (⅔ oz/20 g) chopped cilantro (fresh coriander)

In a saucepan over high heat, combine garlic, lemongrass or lemon zest, chili paste, fish sauce, lemon juice, vinegar and sugar. Bring to a boil, reduce heat to low and simmer, covered, to blend flavors, about 10 minutes.

Stir cornstarch and water into sauce, raise heat to medium and cook, stirring, until sauce is thickened, 2–3 minutes.

Sauce can be stored in airtight container in refrigerator for up to 7 days.

Dashi

4½ cups (36 fl oz/1.1 L) water
1 piece konbu, 4 inches (10 cm) square
2 cups (½ oz/15 g) bonito flakes

Dashi is the base for many Japanese soups. While instant dashi is readily available and has an excellent flavor, the preparation of dashi in the traditional manner offers a superior result. The brand of instant dashi favored most by Japanese is "Aji No Moto hond-ashi."

Wipe surface of konbu with a damp cloth. Place in a saucepan with water and soak for approximately 2 hours. Bring saucepan with soaked konbu to a rapid simmer over high heat. After 5 minutes, check center of konbu and if it is soft, remove from pan. If it is still hard, cook a little longer, then remove. Let return to a boil. Skim any scum from surface. Remove saucepan from heat, and add a little cold water to lower temperature before adding bonito flakes. Do not stir flakes but push them to bottom of pan. Let stand for 3 minutes. Strain through cheesecloth-lined colander, into a bowl.

Fish sauce with chilies

Makes about 1½ cups (12 fl oz/375 ml)

1 cup (8 fl oz/250 ml) fish sauce
1 cup (5 oz/150 g) thinly sliced, fresh medium
   red or green chilies
cloves from ½ bulb garlic, finely chopped
2–3 tablespoons fresh lime juice to taste

In a small bowl or screw-top jar, combine all ingredients,
stir or shake to blend, and serve. Refrigerate, covered, for
several days.

Tip

This is the ubiquitous table seasoning of Thailand, used as
commonly as salt and pepper. For a less spicy sauce, halve
the chilies lengthwise and scrape away some or all of the
seeds. Then thinly slice the chilies as above and continue.

Chili oil

Makes about 1 cup (8 fl oz/250 ml)

¾ cup (6 fl oz/180 ml) vegetable oil
½ cup dried chili flakes

In a well-ventilated room, heat oil in a wok or small, heavy
saucepan over medium to medium–high heat, just until
surface shimmers. Add chili flakes. Stir briefly and
immediately remove from heat. Let cool. If tightly covered,
chili oil will keep indefinitely at room temperature.

Pictured above
Front: Fish sauce with chillies
Back: Chili oil

Coconut cream, milk and water

Choose a good-quality coconut by shaking it to see if it is full of water. If there is none present, discard coconut. If the coconut flesh has spoiled or dried, it will rattle slightly. Hold coconut in your hand, resting it in a heavy tea towel, and use a large knife or small machete to crack coconut by scoring lightly across its circumference. Strike sharply with knife to crack shell. Insert the blade into the crack to pry apart. Take extra care lest you cut your hand. Alternatively, drop coconut onto a hard concrete surface, or use a hammer.

Use a small hand grater to scrape out coconut meat in shreds. Alternatively, place shells in a moderate oven for 15–20 minutes. The flesh will shrink slightly, facilitating removal of the coconut matter. Grate in a food processor.

Put grated coconut in a tea towel and wring it tightly, or put it in a sieve and press it firmly with the back of a large spoon to extract cream; reserve liquid. A chinois sieve, or China cap, works well here.

Add just enough warm or hot water to cover shredded coconut, and press it again to extract thick coconut milk. Repeat again to extract thin coconut milk.

Canned coconut milk or cream can be substituted for fresh. Be sure not to use sweetened coconut milk or cream.

Generally speaking, the less the can shakes, the richer the coconut milk. However, just before using, take care not to shake can. Open carefully and spoon off richest portion (refrigeration facilitates this step) to separate it from the thinner coconut milk.

The liquid sloshing inside the coconut is coconut water, not to be confused with its milk or cream. A young coconut with immature flesh holds the greatest volume of coconut water, but only a fully mature coconut should be used for extracting cream or milk from grated meat.

Garam masala

Makes about ¼ cup (2 fl oz/60 ml)

1 tablespoon cardamom seeds (not pods)
2 cinnamon sticks, broken up
1 teaspoon black peppercorns
1 teaspoon cloves
1 teaspoon cumin seeds
1 teaspoon fennel seeds

In a small skillet, combine all ingredients and stir over medium heat for about 1 minute, or until fragrant. Empty into a bowl and let cool. Transfer to a spice or coffee grinder and grind to a fine powder. Store in a tightly sealed jar in a cool, dark place for up to 4 weeks.

Penang curry paste

Makes about ½ cup (4 fl oz/125 ml)

8 dried red chilies
¼ cup (2 fl oz/60 ml) boiling water
4 scallions (shallots/spring onions)
6 cloves garlic, chopped
2 stalks lemongrass (white part only), chopped
3 cilantro (fresh coriander) roots, coarsely chopped
1 tablespoon peeled and grated fresh ginger
1 teaspoon ground coriander
1 teaspoon ground cumin
2 tablespoons roasted peanuts
2 tablespoons vegetable oil

Put chilies in a small bowl and add boiling water to cover. Let soak for 5 minutes. Drain. Chop chilies coarsely. Transfer to a food processor and add all remaining ingredients. Process to a thick paste. Spoon into a sterilized jar and seal. Store in the refrigerator for up to 3 weeks.

Teriyaki sauce

1 cup (8 fl oz/250 ml) soy sauce
1 cup (7 oz/220 g) brown sugar
2 tablespoons chicken stock (see page 220)
1 teaspoon mirin

In a saucepan over high heat, combine all ingredients and bring to a boil. Simmer for 5 minutes, being careful not to let sauce boil over. Serve hot. Keeps well for up to 2 months in refrigerator.

Front: Garam masala
Back: Penang curry paste

Garlic dipping sauce

Makes ½ cup (4 fl oz/125 ml)

3 tablespoons soy sauce

2 tablespoons Worcestershire sauce

1 tablespoon Asian sesame oil

4 cloves garlic, finely chopped

1 tablespoon superfine (caster) sugar

In a bowl, combine soy sauce, Worcestershire sauce, sesame oil, garlic and sugar. Stir until sugar dissolves. Cover and chill before serving.

Hot chili sauce

Makes 1 cup (8 fl oz/250 ml)

2 lb (1 kg) ripe tomatoes, quartered

3 small dried red chilies, split and seeded

4 tablespoons boiling water

1 tablespoon olive oil

1 onion, finely chopped

1 clove garlic, crushed

olive oil (optional)

Place tomatoes in heavy-bottomed saucepan over low heat and cook stirring occasionally, until they break down and form sauce, about 1 hour. Add a little water if mixture begins to stick. Press through a sieve, set over bowl. (Do not use food processor, as skins need to be removed after tomatoes are cooked.) Set aside.

Place chilies in bowl, add boiling water and let stand 10 minutes. Remove from water and chop; reserve 1 tablespoon of water. Place chilies and reserved water in food processor and process until smooth. Set aside.

In a wok or frying pan, warm oil over medium–high heat. Add onion and cook until softened, about 2 minutes. Add garlic and cook until aromatic, about 1 minute. Reduce heat to low and stir in chili purée. Add tomato pulp and cook until thickened, about 5 minutes. Remove from heat and let cool.

Pour into airtight container and refrigerate until ready to serve. To store for up to 3 weeks, drizzle film of olive oil over top of sauce.

Hot chili sauce

Mango, papaya and green chili relish

Serves 4

1 small ripe mango, peeled, pitted and chopped
¼ small papaya, peeled, seeded and chopped
½ long green chili, seeded and finely chopped
6 scallions (shallots/spring onions), sliced
1 kaffir lime leaf, finely shredded or ½ teaspoon grated lime zest (rind)
3 tablespoons fresh lime juice
2 teaspoons Asian sesame oil

In a small bowl, combine mango, papaya, chili, scallions and lime leaf. Stir in lime juice and sesame oil. Mix well. Cover and chill for 30 minutes.

Massaman curry paste

Makes about ¾ cup (6 fl oz/180 ml)

8 dried long red chilies, seeded
¼ cup (20 g) coriander seeds
2 tablespoons cumin seeds
4 star anise pods, crushed
2 cinnamon quills, broken
10 cloves
1 teaspoon salt
⅔ cup (5 fl oz/150 ml) vegetable oil
6 large cloves garlic, crushed
2 tablespoons finely chopped shallots (French shallots), preferably pink
6 thin slices galangal, chopped
1 stalk lemongrass, white part only, peeled and chopped
1 teaspoon chopped kaffir lime zest (rind)

Soak dried chilies in warm water for 10 minutes. Drain and pat dry. In a small frying pan over medium heat, separately toast each spice, stirring constantly, until fragrant. Immediately remove from heat and pour spices into a large mortar or spice grinder. Add salt and grind to a fine powder. Transfer to a small bowl.

In a wok or large, heavy frying pan, heat oil over medium–high heat. Add the garlic, shallots, and drained chilies. Fry until slightly golden, 1–2 minutes. Remove with a slotted spoon, reserve solids and discard oil. Add galangal, lemongrass, and kaffir lime zest to a large mortar, and pound to a paste, 10–20 minutes. Halfway through, add fried garlic, shallots, and chilies and pound until smooth. Add ground spices. Alternatively, grind dried spices then coarsely chop fresh ingredients, and place them in a food processor and process until finely chopped. If necessary, add a small amount of water, 1 teaspoon at a time.

Mint Raita

Serves 8

½ cup (¾ oz/20 g) coarsely chopped fresh mint

½ cup (¾ oz/20 g) coarsely chopped cilantro (fresh coriander)

4 teaspoons finely grated fresh ginger

2 teaspoons finely chopped fresh green chili

1 cup (8 oz/250 g) plain (natural) whole-milk yogurt

salt to taste

In a food processor, combine mint, cilantro, ginger and chili and process until finely chopped.

In a bowl, whisk yogurt. Add chopped mint mixture and mix well. Season with salt.

Note: Raitas are based on yogurt, which is whipped or whisked. You can use either whole-milk (full-fat) or reduced-fat yogurt. This raita can be made 1 day ahead. Store in an airtight container in refrigerator.

Nuoc cham nem sauce

Makes about 2 cups (16 fl oz/500 ml)

3 cloves garlic

1 fresh long red chili, seeded

½ cup (4 fl oz/125 ml) fish sauce

¼ cup (2 fl oz/60 ml) rice vinegar or distilled white vinegar

⅔ cup (5 fl oz/160 ml) water

3–4 tablespoons sugar to taste

1 carrot, peeled and finely shredded or chopped

½ cup (2 oz/60 g) peeled and shredded and chopped green papaya

½ teaspoon ground pepper

In a mortar, pound garlic and chili with a pestle to a paste. Stir in fish sauce, vinegar, water and sugar, and continue stirring until sugar is dissolved. Alternatively, in a blender or food processor, combine garlic, chili, fish sauce, vinegar, water and sugar and purée. Stir in shredded carrot, papaya and pepper.

Tips

- This sauce is best consumed on the day it is made, or the day after.
- If green papaya is unavailable, substitute shredded, peeled daikon (giant white radish) or jicama (yam bean). Shredded daikon smells strongly if not used within a few hours.

Paneer

4 qt (4 L) whole (full cream) milk
1⅔ cups (13 fl oz/400 ml) heavy (double) cream
⅔ cup (5 fl oz/150 ml) white vinegar

Line a large, flat-bottomed sieve with a double layer of cheesecloth (muslin), allowing it to overhang sides of sieve. Place lined sieve inside a large other bowl. Choose a large, heavy, non-aluminum saucepan that fits inside the sieve.

Pour milk into the saucepan and bring slowly to a boil over medium heat. When milk is almost boiling, stir in cream and bring to a boil again. When milk mixture just comes to a boil (it will begin to bubble and froth, and vibrations from boiling mixture can be felt in the handle of a metal spoon held in milk), pour in vinegar and remove from heat. Set aside for 2 minutes; do not stir.

Using a large slotted spoon or spoon-shaped strainer, gently lift curds from whey and place in lined sieve.

Once all curds have been placed in sieve, carefully tie loose ends of cheesecloth together to form curds into a thick, round disk about 10 inches (25 cm) in diameter.

Return whey in bowl back to saucepan holding remainder of whey. Place saucepan on top of paneer to weight it. Set aside at room temperature until paneer is firm, about 25 minutes.

Remove saucepan from paneer. Carefully untie cheesecloth and remove paneer. Prepare as directed in individual recipes. If not using paneer immediately, place flat in an airtight container and add enough whey to cover. Store in refrigerator for up to 1 week.

Sambal oelek

Makes about 1½ cups (12 fl oz/375 ml)

1 lb (500 g) red chilies
2½ cups water (20 fl oz/625 ml)
1 tablespoon white vinegar
1 teaspoon superfine (caster) sugar
2 tablespoons peanut oil
½ cup (4 fl oz/125 ml) boiling water

This mixture of red chilies, vinegar and salt is used throughout Asian cooking as a flavoring and as a spicy hot condiment.

Remove stems from chilies. Remove seeds if you want less fiery sambal oelek. Place chilies and water in a saucepan over medium heat and bring to a boil. Cover, reduce heat to simmer and cook until chilies are soft, about 15 minutes. Drain. Working in batches, place chilies in a food processor and process until smooth. Add vinegar, sugar, peanut oil and boiling water and process to combine. Pour into sterilized jars, seal and refrigerate for up to 1 month.

Tahini Sauce

Makes 1½ cups (12 fl oz/375 ml)

2 cloves garlic
½ teaspoon salt, plus extra salt to taste
¾ cup (6 fl oz/185 ml) tahini
⅓ cup (3 fl oz/90 ml) cold water
⅓ cup (3 fl oz/90 ml) lemon juice

In a small bowl, crush garlic with ½ teaspoon salt and mix to a paste. Gradually add tahini, beating well with a wooden spoon.

Then alternately beat in small amounts of water and lemon juice. The water will thicken the mixture; lemon juice will thin it. Add all the lemon juice, and enough water to give the sauce a thin or thick consistency, depending on use. The flavor should be tart. Add salt to taste if necessary. Use the sauce as a dip with pita bread or as an accompaniment for falafel, fried or poached fish, or boiled cauliflower or potatoes.

Food processor method: Place tahini and garlic in processor bowl and process for a few seconds to crush garlic. Add lemon juice and water alternately, a small amount at a time, until desired consistency is reached. Blend in salt to taste.

Green curry paste

Makes about 1½ cups (12 fl oz/375 ml)

1 tablespoon coriander seeds
1 tablespoon cumin seeds
4 black peppercorns
1 cup (1⅓ oz/40 g) coarsely chopped cilantro (fresh
   coriander)
2 fresh kaffir lime leaves, shredded
6 cloves garlic, chopped
4 scallions (shallots/spring onions), including green
   parts, coarsely chopped
4 fresh green Thai or Anaheim chilies, seeded and
   coarsely chopped
1 tablespoon grated fresh galangal
1 teaspoon dried shrimp paste
2 stalks lemongrass, white part only, chopped
2 teaspoons fish sauce
2 tablespoons vegetable oil

In a wok or small frying pan, combine coriander, cumin and peppercorns and stir over medium heat until fragrant, about 1 minute. Empty into a bowl and let cool. Transfer to a spice or coffee grinder and grind to a fine powder. Transfer to a food processor and add remaining ingredients. Process to a smooth paste. Spoon into a sterilized jar and seal. Store in the refrigerator for up to 3 weeks.

Tips

• Green Thai chilies are medium–hot and grow up to 1½ inches (4 cm) long. The green Anaheim chili is somewhat milder, similarly shaped and grows up to 6 inches (15 cm) long.
• Bird's eye chilies are blazing hot, with a clear fiery taste. These small green or red chilies, about ½ inch (12 mm) long, should be used in small quantities.

Red curry paste

Makes about 1 cup (8 fl oz/250 ml)

6 red bird's eye or Thai chilies, seeded
   and coarsely chopped
2 teaspoons black peppercorns
2 teaspoons cumin seeds
1 teaspoon sweet paprika
1 teaspoon dried shrimp paste
1 red onion, coarsely chopped
2 stalks lemongrass, white part only, chopped
4 cloves garlic, chopped
1 tablespoon grated fresh galangal
2 tablespoons coarsely chopped cilantro (fresh
   coriander)
2 tablespoons vegetable oil
2 teaspoons fish sauce

In a wok or small frying pan, combine chilies, peppercorns, cumin seeds, paprika and shrimp paste and stir over medium heat until fragrant, 30–60 seconds. Remove from heat and let cool. Transfer to a food processor. Add remaining ingredients and process to a smooth paste. Spoon into a sterilized jar and seal. Store in the refrigerator for up to 3 weeks.

Front: Thai red curry paste
Back: Thai green curry paste

Thai chili dipping sauce

Makes about 1 cup (8 fl oz/250 ml)

15 fresh long green chilies, roasted
1 whole bulb garlic
9 shallots (French shallots), about 3 oz (100 g),
   preferably pink
¼ teaspoon dried shrimp paste
½ teaspoon salt
1 tablespoon fish sauce

Peel and stem the roasted chilies but retain seeds. (For a less piquant sauce, discard some or all of the seeds.) Preheat oven to 400°F (200°C). Lightly break unpeeled garlic bulb by pressing on a knife handle with the heel of your hand, so that the cloves sit loosely together; do not separate cloves from bulb completely. Separately wrap the garlic and shallots in aluminum foil. Roast on the top shelf of the oven for about 30 minutes, or until soft to touch. Remove from oven and allow to cool to touch in foil. Peel shallots and garlic (you should have about ⅓ cup (1½ oz/45 g) shallots).

In a mortar, pound chilies gently with a pestle to break them up. Add garlic, and pound briefly, then add shallots. Add shrimp paste and salt and pound again to a coarse paste. Or, pulse ingredients in a food processor. Stir in fish sauce. Serve with a selection of vegetable crudités.

Tomato salsa
with chili and cilantro

Serves 4–6

2 large vine-ripened tomatoes, chopped
1 small red chili, seeded and chopped
½ small red (Spanish) onion, chopped
⅓ cup (½ oz/10 g) chopped cilantro (fresh coriander)
2 tablespoons balsamic vinegar
1 tablespoon fresh lime juice
sea salt and freshly ground black pepper

In a bowl, combine tomatoes, chili, onion and cilantro. Combine balsamic vinegar and lime juice in a small bowl, mix well and add to tomato mixture. Stir and season with salt and pepper. Cover and allow to stand at room temperature for 15 minutes before serving.

Tips
- The salsa is excellent with hot-and-spicy money bags, poultry, chili-noodle cakes and shrimp. It also makes a delicious accompaniment for fried wontons and grilled fish or chicken.
- Bird's eye or serrano chilies are recommended for this recipe.

Glossary

Acacia: Pungent smelling feathery light-green leaves, with a spiky stalk and sometimes tiny white flowers. Available in Southeast Asian markets.

Asian sesame oil: Rich, dark- or golden-colored oil extracted from sesame seeds. Oil made from toasted seeds has a pronounced nutty flavor.

Bamboo leaves: Long, narrow leaves available dried from Asian food stores. Leaves impart subtle flavor to food, but are not eaten. Soak briefly in boiling water to soften before use.

Bamboo shoots: Young shoots of a tropical plant, which are boiled to retain their sweet flavor. Most commonly found canned, packed in water.

Banana leaves: Large leaves from the banana plant, used to line bamboo steamers or for wrapping foods prior to steaming. Parchment (baking) paper may be substituted. The leaves are available fresh or frozen.

Bean sprouts: Sprouted beans and peas add a fresh flavor and crunchy texture to salads and other Asian dishes. Mung bean sprouts are sold fresh or canned. Snow pea (mange-tout) sprouts are available fresh. Fresh sprouts are preferred for their clean taste and crisp texture; store in refrigerator for up to 3 days.

Besan flour: A pale yellow flour made from chickpeas. Available from health food stores.

Bok choy: Asian variety of cabbage with dark green leaves and thick white stems. Sizes vary from baby bok choy about 6 inches (15 cm) long to bok choy as long as a celery stalk.

Cellophane noodles: Thin translucent dried noodles made from mung bean starch and sold in bundles. Also called bean thread noodles.

Chili oil: Spicy oil produced by steeping red chilies in oil. It is available bottled or you can prepare your own (see page 223).

Chili paste: Fiery condiment made from ground red chilies and sometimes garlic. Use in small quantities.

Chilies: As a general rule, the smaller the chili the hotter it is. For a milder taste, remove the seeds and membrane of chili before adding to dishes. Dried chili flakes and chili powder can be substituted.

Chinese broccoli: Broccoli with white flowers and a bitter taste. Also known as gai laan. Sometimes confused with choy sum. Chinese broccoli and choy sum can be used in place of each other.

Chinese celery: Straggly and sparse in appearance compared to standard celery, Chinese celery is also a darker green and more pronounced in flavor. Use both the stems and leaves.

Chinese dried mushrooms: Intensely flavorful, dark mushrooms that need to be rehydrated before use. The stems are discarded. Flavorful fresh mushrooms make an acceptable substitute.

Chinese five-spice powder: This is made of an equal mixture of ground Szechuan peppercorns, star anise, fennel, cloves and cinnamon. Available at most supermarkets.

Chinese sausages: These dried, long, thin sausages are sold unrefrigerated in Asian markets by their Chinese name, "lop chong." Made of seasoned pork, they are slightly sweet and are added to stir-fries or steamed.

Choy sum: Also known as flowering cabbage, this mild-flavored Chinese green has thin stalks bearing leaves and yellow flowers, all of which are used in cooking.

Cilantro (fresh coriander): The fresh leaf, stem and root of the coriander plant. Both stems and leaves are commonly chopped and added to food, and sprigs are used as garnish and served at the table as an accompaniment or table green. Also known as Chinese parsley.

Coconut milk and cream: These are made from grated coconut flesh (not the liquid inside coconuts). Thicker coconut cream adds more flavor than the thinner coconut milk. Available in cans from supermarkets or you can prepare your own (see page 224).

Coriander seeds: The tiny yellow-tan seeds of the cilantro (coriander) plant. Used whole or ground as a spice.

Cumin: Also known as comino. The small crescent-shaped seeds have an earthy, nutty flavor. Available whole or ground.

Curry paste: Condiment consisting of curry seasonings and red or green chilies. Both red and green curry pastes are available bottled, or you may make your own versions (see page 231).

Dashi: Japanese fish broth made from dried bonito fish flakes (katsuobushi) and konbu/kombu (a seaweed). Available in concentrated liquid, powder or dried granules, or you may make your own (see page 222).

Fenugreek: The seed of an aromatic plant of the pea family, native to the Mediterranean region. Has a bitter-sweet, burnt sugar aftertaste, available whole or ground.

Fish sauce: Also known as nam pla, nuoc nam and patis, this distinctive, salty sauce is made from fermented shrimp or fish and is used similarly to soy sauce to enhance and balance the flavor of dishes. Some are much saltier than others; use sparingly and add to taste.

Five-spice powder: A mixture of five spices of equal parts—cinnamon, cloves, fennel seed, star anise and Szechuan pepper.

Flat-leaf parsley: Parsley with a flat leaf and stronger flavor than curly-leaf parsley. Also known as Italian or Continental parsley. Fresh parsley can be stored for up to 1 week in a plastic bag in the refrigerator.

Flowering cabbage: See Choy sum.

Garam masala: A blend of spices—cardamom, cumin, coriander, cinnamon, cloves and pepper. Store away from sunlight. (See page 225 for recipe.)

Ghee: A form of clarified fat or pure butter fat, originating in India. Has a high smoke point and nutty, caramel-like flavor.

Ginger: Thick rootlike rhizome of the ginger plant with a sharp, pungent flavor. Once the thin tan skin is peeled away from fresh ginger, the flesh is grated and used in sauces, marinades, stir-fries and dressings, or is sliced, bruised and added to stocks and soups. Store fresh ginger in refrigerator for 2–3 days.

Green papaya: Unripe papaya used grated in Asian cooking. Because it is very sticky, oil your hands or wear gloves and oil the grater before preparing.

Hokkien noodles: Fat, round, thick wheat noodles, usually dark yellow and available fresh from Asian stores.

Kaffir lime: The distinctive fragrant double leaves and fruit of this Asian tree are increasingly available fresh from Asian and many Western supermarkets. Frozen and dried leaves and frozen fruit are also available but lack the flavor of the fresh.

Lemongrass: A popular lemon-scented grass used in Asian-style dishes. Use only the white part or the bulb. Trim the root and remove the outer layer. Chop finely or bruise by hitting with a meat mallet or blunt side of a chef's knife to bring out the flavor.

Long bean: Related to the black-eyed pea, this thin, flexible but crisp-textured green bean is cut into short lengths before cooking. Long beans are also called snake beans and yard-long beans, though most found in markets are 24 inches (60 cm) or less in length.

Massaman curry paste: A mild curry paste with a hint of cinnamon, nutmeg and cloves. Not as hot as Thai green or red curry paste.

Mirin: A sweet Japanese rice wine used for cooking. Sweet sherry can be substituted.

Miso: Thick paste of fermented ground soybeans, used in Japanese soups and other dishes. Light-colored varieties of miso are milder in flavor than dark-colored pastes.

Mizuna: A feathery Japanese salad green with a delicate flavor.

Mushrooms, tree ear or cloud (black or white fungus): These add texture, but little taste, to food, but absorb flavors during cooking. The dried mushrooms must be soaked in water to rehydrate, then rinsed thoroughly and drained. Trim the tough stems from the fresh or dried mushrooms before using.

Nam pla: See Fish sauce.

Oyster mushrooms: Creamy white mushrooms with fanshaped caps, named for their resemblance to an oyster. Possessing a very mild, delicate flavor, oyster mushrooms grow in the wild and are cultivated. Available fresh in well stocked supermarkets and produce markets. Substitute button mushrooms if unavailable.

Paprika: A blend of dried red skinned chilies. The flavor can range from slightly sweet and mild to pungent and hot.

Rice wine: Sweet, low-alcohol Chinese wine, also known as shaoxing wine, made from fermented glutinous rice. Sake or dry sherry can be substituted.

Sambal oelek: Indonesian paste consisting of ground chilies combined with salt and occasionally vinegar. This spicy condiment is available bottled, or you can prepare your own (see page 230).

Shaoxing wine: See rice wine.

Shiso: Aromatic green, jagged-edged leaf from the perilla plant, which is part of the mint and basil family. Shiso leaves are used in salads, cooked dishes such as tempura, and as a garnish. Shiso leaves are available fresh from Asian markets.

Shrimp paste: Produced by drying, salting and pounding shrimp into a pungent-flavored paste that is then formed into blocks or cakes.

Soy sauce: Salty sauce made from soybeans and used both as an ingredient and as a table condiment. Dark soy sauce, usually used in cooking, is thicker and often less salty than light soy sauce, which is added to dipping sauces. Low-sodium products are also available.

Star anise: The dried eight-pointed star-shaped seed pod of a tree belonging to the magnolia family. Star anise is one of the ingredients of Chinese five spice powder. It is also used whole, in segments or ground in Asian cooking. It has an intense liquorice flavor.

Sweet chili sauce: Use as a dipping sauce or combine with other sauces, such as soy, plum or ketjap manis. May also contain garlic and/or ginger. Hotter and less-sweet chili sauces may be substituted.

Tahini (sesame paste): A smooth paste made from ground sesame seeds. Some are thicker than others, so add extra water if required. Available from most supermarkets.

Tamarind pulp: Available as powder, paste or pulp, this popular Asian fruit adds a sour flavor. Soak pulp required in hot water for about 15 minutes, then push through a fine-mesh sieve to extract the liquid, discarding the pulp. Dissolve powders and pastes before use, but be aware that some can be quite salty.

Tikka masala curry paste: A mild curry paste. Other curry pastes can be substituted.

Tofu: Produced from soybeans that have been dried, soaked, cooked, puréed and pressed to form cakes or squares that range in texture from soft to firm. Mild in flavor, tofu readily absorbs the seasonings of the preparations in which it is used.

Turmeric: A dried, powdery spice produced from the rhizome of a tropical plant related to ginger. It has a strong, spicy flavor and yellow color. Also known as Indian saffron.

Vermicelli noodles: Very thin noodles made of rice flour. Sometimes referred to as cellophane noodles. Available dried in Asian food stores and supermarkets.

Index

guide to weights and measures

The conversions given in the recipes in this book are approximate. Whichever system you use, remember to follow it consistently, thereby ensuring that the proportions are consistent throughout a recipe.

Weights

Imperial	Metric
1/3 oz	10 g
1/2 oz	15 g
3/4 oz	20 g
1 oz	30 g
2 oz	60 g
3 oz	90 g
4 oz (1/4 lb)	125 g
5 oz (1/3 lb)	150 g
6 oz	180 g
7 oz	220 g
8 oz (1/2 lb)	250 g
9 oz	280 g
10 oz	300 g
11 oz	330 g
12 oz (3/4 lb)	375 g
16 oz (1 lb)	500 g
2 lb	1 kg
3 lb	1.5 kg
4 lb	2 kg

Volume

Imperial	Metric	Cup
1 fl oz	30 ml	
2 fl oz	60 ml	1/4
3 fl oz	90 ml	1/3
4 fl oz	125 ml	1/2
5 fl oz	150 ml	2/3
6 fl oz	180 ml	3/4
8 fl oz	250 ml	1
10 fl oz	300 ml	1 1/4
12 fl oz	375 ml	1 1/2
13 fl oz	400 ml	1 2/3
14 fl oz	440 ml	1 3/4
16 fl oz	500 ml	2
24 fl oz	750 ml	3
32 fl oz	1L	4

Oven temperature guide

The Celsius (°C) and Fahrenheit (°F) temperatures in this chart apply to most electric ovens. Decrease by 25°F or 10°C for a gas oven or refer to the manufacturer's temperature guide. For temperatures below 325°F (160°C), do not decrease the given temperature.

Oven description	°C	°F	Gas Mark
Cool	110	225	1/4
	130	250	1/2
Very slow	140	275	1
	150	300	2
Slow	170	325	3
Moderate	180	350	4
	190	375	5
Moderately Hot	200	400	6
Fairly Hot	220	425	7
Hot	230	450	8
Very Hot	240	475	9
Extremely Hot	250	500	10

Useful conversions

1/4 teaspoon	1.25 ml
1/2 teaspoon	2.5 ml
1 teaspoon	5 ml
1 Australian tablespoon	20 ml (4 teaspoons)
1 UK/US tablespoon	15 ml (3 teaspoons)

Butter/Shortening

1 tablespoon	1/2 oz	15 g
1 1/2 tablespoons	3/4 oz	20 g
2 tablespoons	1 oz	30 g
3 tablespoons	1 1/2 oz	45 g

A LANSDOWNE BOOK

Published by Apple Press in 2005
Sheridan House
4th Floor
112-116 Western Road
Hove
East Sussex BN3 1DD UK

www.apple-press.com

Created and produced by Lansdowne Publishing Pty Ltd
Principal contributor: Vicki Liley
Contributors: Katharine Blakemore, Robert Carmack, Soon Young Choong, Didier Corlou,
   Shunsuke Fukushima, Bettina Jenkins, Ajoy Joshi, Sompon Nabnian, Jacki Passmore,
   Jan Purser, Suzie Smith, Brigid Treloar, Nguyen Thanh Van, Rosemary Wadey
Design: Avril Makula
Photography: Quentin Bacon, Alan Benson, Ben Dearnley, Andrew Elton, Chris Jones,
   Vicky Liley, Louise Lister, Andre Martin
Editor: Joanne Holliman
Production: Sally Stokes and Eleanor Cant
Project Co-ordinator: Kate Merrifield

ISBN-10: 1 84543 067 0
ISBN-13: 978 1 84543 067 2

Set in Helvetica on QuarkXPress
Printed in Singapore by Tien Wah Press (Pte) Ltd.